EPI

Gaby Deslys

A FATAL ATTRACTION

Gaby Deslys
A FATAL ATTRACTION

JAMES GARDINER

SIDGWICK & JACKSON
LONDON

To Gabrielle Irving

First published in 1986 in Great Britain by
Sidgwick and Jackson Limited

Copyright © 1986 by James Gardiner

ISBN 0-283-99398-7

Typeset by Hewer Text Composition Services, Edinburgh

Printed by The Garden City Press
for Sidgwick and Jackson Limited,
1 Tavistock Chambers, Bloomsbury Way
London WC1A 2SG

CONTENTS

	Acknowledgements	vii
	Foreword	ix
	Prologue	xi
1	The Wrong Ambitions	1
2	Night Classes	8
3	Gaiety Girl	18
4	Applause and Champagne	25
5	The Most Talked About Woman in the World	30
6	Altered Values	47
7	The Tiger and the Butterfly	55
8	No Honeymoon	64
9	A Question of Decency	77
10	The Freak Show	90
11	A Hundred Pounds a Night	97
12	The Right Connections	103
13	5064 Gerrard	114
14	Private Feelings	121
15	Public Property	130
16	Let 'em Fall!	149
17	The Ladders of Victory	159
18	A Fatal Attraction	168
19	A Macabre and Ridiculous Joke	181
	Epilogue	189
	Index	191

ACKNOWLEDGEMENTS

In this book I have attempted to cast some light on the life and character of one of the most colourful theatrical personalities of her time, and, alas, one of the most neglected since her premature death over sixty-five years ago.

Researching the details of Gaby Deslys' brief life and fitting them together into an accurate picture has not been an easy task. If I have succeeded at all it has only been with the help of many who have been generous with their time, shared their memories, and pointed me in the right direction.

I am therefore greatly indebted to the following individuals and organizations: Richard Aisbitt, the late Ellis Ashton, Richard Bebb, Dr Arthur A. Bradley, Samson de Brier, Douglas Byng, Madame Brun of the Conservatoire de Musique, Marseilles, Gérard Caire, La Cinématèque Française, Ruth Edge and Chris Ellis of EMI, Erté, Claire Luce, The Raymond Mander and Joe Mitchenson Theatre Collection, Leela Meinertas at the Theatre Museum, Madame Messinesi, Robert Nesbitt, Steve Race, Charles Spencer, Hugo Vickers, Victor Yates of Selfridges, the staff of the British Library Newspaper Library, the staff of the Bibliothèque de l'Arsenal, Selfridges for allowing me to reproduce the photograph of Gordon Selfridge, the John Hillelson Agency for allowing me to reproduce Lartigue's photographs, the Theatre Museum and the British Library for permission to reproduce photographs from their collections, Mrs Salome Estorick of the Grosvenor Gallery for allowing me to reproduce Erté's design for Gaby Deslys on the back of the jacket.

A special debt of gratitude is owed to:
Barbara Butler for instilling in me the confidence to proceed with this project; John Taylor, Maurice Seure and Dennis O'Sullivan for their tireless researches; Elaine Causon for typing the many drafts;

John Jesse and Irina Laski for allowing me to reproduce photographs from their collection; Kendal Duesbury for all his advice, and Patrick O'Connor for his; my editors Susan Hill and Jane MacAndrew for their invaluable guidance; Alan and Elizabeth Ward for their hospitality; Gabrielle Castillo for her encouragement and enthusiasm and Trevor Davey for his inexhaustible patience.

FOREWORD

I met Gaby Deslys for the first time in 1919 at Monte Carlo where I was living then. She came to ask me to design some costumes for her to wear in a revue that Madame Rasimi was about to stage at the Fémina Theatre in Paris. This revue was called *La Marche à l'Étoile*, and the 'Star' of the title was Gaby herself. She was indeed the greatest star of the music hall, with all the appropriate qualities. Ravishing to look at, she sang charmingly, and danced to perfection with her partner Harry Pilcer. She was as likeable and kind as she was beautiful, and I have wonderful memories of her. She originated the elaborate feathered costumes of music-hall revue: Mistinguett and all those who came later were but imitators of her unique allure.

What a pity that her life and career were cut so tragically short.

I am so glad that a book about her is finally appearing, and hope that these words will help her live again.

Erté

Boulogne sur Seine
June 1986

PROLOGUE

Rue Henri-de-Bornier is a quiet back street in the sixteenth *arrondissement* of Paris. Situated on the edge of the Bois de Boulogne, it once formed a part of the city's most exclusive residential area. Today, however, few people can afford to live in the mansions and large terraced town houses whose proud façades dominate these streets. Brass plaques that once bore the names of the French upper crust have long since gone, having been replaced by those of the various embassies and consulates that are now situated here.

One of the smallest houses in the street is number three. Tacked onto the end of a terrace, its Art-Nouveau detailing distinguishes it from its older and larger neighbours. Long before the foreign envoys and their attendant guards arrived here, on the morning of 14 February 1920, this house was the unlikely focus of world attention. At nine o'clock that morning, a funeral cortège began to assemble here; a cortège of such proportions that it proclaimed the death of no ordinary mortal. For the preceding two days flowers had arrived continuously: vast wreaths from organizations and wealthy individuals; smaller bouquets from poorer folk, domestic servants, shop girls, even children, all of whose lives had in some way been touched by the woman who had lived here. It was hard to imagine where so many flowers could have come from. All the hot houses of France must have been plundered, such was the profusion of lilac, roses, orchids, tulips and lilies – so many lilies. For this was the flower that held special significance for the dead woman, the flower whose name she bore: Gabrielle of the Lilies, Gaby Deslys.

At ten o'clock the procession left the house led by two carriages, each drawn by a pair of black horses, their bridles surmounted by black feathers and emblazoned with gold monograms of the initials G.D. The first carriage contained the carved mahogany coffin.

Its handles and the crucifix on its lid were of silver, and it was draped with a white satin cloth embroidered with purple orchids. The vehicle in which it rested was overflowing with wreaths and floral tributes, scores more of which were placed in the second carriage: the *char de couronnes*, whose sole purpose it was to carry them. The third vehicle in the procession was a long, sleek, white automobile, a thirty-horsepower 'Sheffield'; a type rarely seen on European streets, being more normally reserved for the 'Heroine-Queens' of American movies. Its shades were pulled down to conceal three distraught occupants, and black drapes blinded its huge chrome headlights. Many more cars followed. As they made their slow progress to the Church of Notre Dame de Grace at Passy, the mourners halted the normal working routine of the neighbourhoods through which they passed. Housewives, shopkeepers and servants stared wide-eyed from windows and doorsteps as the procession made its way to the little church, around which a crowd of thousands was gathering.

The crowd was so dense by the time the cortège arrived that the pallbearers had difficulty getting the coffin and the principal mourners into the church. The whole of the French theatre world seemed to be there; great actors and actresses, directors, writers, choreographers, theatre managers and owners, as well as hundreds of chorus boys and girls, musicians, stagehands – all who had counted this woman a friend.

And yet, so few of them had really known her. She had lived most of her life in the glare of publicity, and yet had revealed so little. After she died, the stories and speculations surrounding her multiplied. Her death itself was something of a mystery. Everyone knew that she had been hospitalized for weeks and had undergone many operations, but nothing else besides.

The official statement concerning her unexpected demise stated that it was caused by 'an affection of the throat', and to this uninformative phrase the press and gossipmongers added their own embellishments. Some newspapers hinted at a 'tumour', some said 'pleurisy', others 'influenza'. But the rumour that spread like wildfire through the theatrical profession, that was whispered in dressing rooms from Montmartre to Shaftesbury Avenue to Broadway, was that syphilis had killed the queen of the music hall.

Scandal had attended her in her lifetime, and would pursue her beyond the grave.

It was a long service. The curate, Father Hennelique, gave a lengthy and moving address. This was an occasion the priest would remember all his life, and he made the most of it. The atmosphere was stifling. It was a cold day; those who could afford them were wrapped in furs, but for everyone who crammed into the little church with the doors firmly shut behind them, and with the heavy, sickly smell of the incense mingled with the perfume of the many flowers, the atmosphere soon became unbearable.

The doors were finally opened, and the church emptied. After a pause, the coffin lid was lifted so that Gaby Deslys' many friends could bid her adieu. The embalmers had done their job well. If she had suffered in the last months of her life, it was not apparent. Her death certificate revealed that she was thirty-six years old, but she looked younger. Although her eyes – once her most expressive feature – were now forever hidden from view, she still looked beautiful, and a faint smile played over her mouth. Around her neck she wore, as she always had, a row of perfectly matched pearls. She looked peaceful, and almost pleased with herself. In death, as in life, she was getting her own way, as was revealed when her will was opened that same afternoon. After various bequests that would later make world headlines, she had written: '. . . and I want a good funeral. Make sure it costs at least twenty-thousand francs.'

The funeral service was just the beginning of the granting of her request. The coffin rested overnight in a side chapel and, the following morning, a special train with a carriage hurriedly made to take it – a carriage with padded and quilted walls of black satin piped with gold – took the coffin and its precious cargo on one last journey – south, to Marseilles.

1
THE WRONG AMBITIONS

Marseilles is a beautiful city. Its wide boulevards slope down to the old port; avenues of plane trees shade the cafés and bustling pavements from the scorching Mediterranean sun. The main thoroughfare, La Canebière, is a thriving marketplace, lined at the end nearest the harbour with grand shops and hotels. As the road climbs gently northwards, the shops become smaller and shabbier. Here, the steep side streets teem with life, but of a seamier nature: unkempt children play street games, north African pedlars ply their dubious wares, gaudily dressed streetwalkers do likewise.

One of these side streets is rue de la Rotonde, a typical French terrace of high houses with elaborate ironwork balconies and small shops at ground level. It is very run-down now, even the 'girls' clustered in doorways, or slowly parading up and down the shady side of the street, seem a little old and tired. Like the buildings, they have seen better days.

When Gabrielle Caire was born at number fifty-three in 1881, it was still a respectable address. Hippolyte Caire and his new bride Anna had moved there soon after their marriage in 1874, when the street was fairly new. The Caire family were well-known in the region. Hippolyte Caire and his brother, Léon, were successful textile merchants, and another brother was mayor of the nearby town of Velaux. Hippolyte had done well, expanding the family business, postponing marriage until, at the age of thirty-three, he felt financially secure enough to support a wife and the inevitable family. The woman he finally chose was Anna Terras, a pretty seventeen-year-old from a poorer family who were happy to see her married to this successful businessman.

Anna had always secretly cherished the idea of going on the stage. This was not, however, a career favoured by poor parents with bourgeois pretensions for their daughters, and so, yielding to

1

family pressure, she married Hippolyte. They settled down happily enough, but in the early years of their marriage this happiness was marred by the death, at the age of thirteen months, of their first-born child, a daughter who had been called Marie-Thérèse after her maternal grandmother. It was a doubly traumatic experience for Anna, for she was already pregnant again. Soon afterwards she gave birth to a boy, who was named Léon after his uncle. Much though both parents loved their son, they longed for another daughter to replace Marie-Thérèse. Hippolyte, particularly, had doted on the little girl, and he was distraught. Three years passed before Anna became pregnant again. She and her husband prayed for a daughter. Their wish was granted with the birth, in 1879, of a little girl who they named Aimée, the loved one. Aimée held a very special place in her parents' affections, especially her father's.

Over the next few years, Anna presented her husband with two more daughters. The first, born on 4 November 1881, was a tiny, fragile baby, with her mother's colouring: golden-brown hair, fair skin, and unusual blue-green-grey eyes. She was baptized Marie-Elise-Gabrielle. Her mother always called her Gaby-Elise, but to most people she was simply 'Gaby'. The youngest, Marie-Jean-Mathilde, was born a year or two later, and as she grew up she became known as Matichon.

It was a noisy household. Anna, a capable mother, coped remarkably well with her brood, but it was nevertheless fortunate that Hippolyte's business was doing sufficiently well for them to afford domestic help. The textile business was flourishing, and several sales representatives travelled on Hippolyte's behalf all over the South of France. Running the organization took up more and more of his time, and sometimes long periods passed when his family hardly saw him. He seemed to get little enjoyment from the money he made, but, as he got older, making more became an overriding preoccupation. The family moved to the boulevard de la Corderie, close to the harbour. There was much more space to bring up the children, and the ground floor was occupied by a large retail shop, with offices behind.

They had barely moved in when, in August 1885, Léon, the Caire's eldest child and only son, died of tuberculosis. The girls were hardly old enough to understand, but their parents were grief-stricken. The boy's death had a disastrous effect on Hippolyte's character. He became increasingly stern with his family and, although his love for his daughters was undiminished, he found it difficult to show affection. Aimée remained his favourite, but even she found it hard to make him smile. He threw himself with renewed vigour into his business, and even expected the household to be run exactly in accordance with his wishes. Nevertheless, he commanded the respect of both his family and his employees, with whom he had the reputation of being a fair, if sombre, man. Despite the rather sad background their father lent to their formative years, his three daughters grew up into perfectly normal, surprisingly high-spirited young women. If he showed them little open affection, their mother compensated for it; she was as warm and loving as he was melancholic and remote.

Of the three girls, Gaby exhibited the strongest character. She was a cheerful extrovert, she loved to show off, and from her earliest years displayed a talent for singing and dancing. This delighted her mother, who saw in her an image of herself when young. The three sisters went everywhere together. Gaby was the ringleader in all the girlish pranks they got up to: dressing in their mother's clothes at every opportunity and, even at the age of twelve or thirteen, letting themselves out of a ground-floor window at night to consort with local boys. This 'consorting' never went further than a few clandestine kisses and cuddles, but naturally, when their parents found out about it they were horrified, and threatened the girls with a beating if it ever happened again.

In an attempt to calm down Gaby's increasing high spirits, her father insisted on arranging for her to receive a strict and pious education, apart from her sisters, at the college of the Dames de St Maur, a convent school fashionable for the daughters of the bourgeoisie. The nuns, however, could do little for her. She was not very bright academically; she was what would now be called 'streetwise'. But the horror of horrors, as far as the nuns of St Maur as well as her father were concerned, was that Gaby wanted to be an actress. A friend of hers at school, Régine Flory, had the same ambitions, and together they shared their hopes of future fame and fortune.

In French polite society of the late nineteenth century, it was completely unacceptable for girls to pursue a stage career. Gaby learned early that, if she wanted to discuss her theatrical ambitions, she could only do so with her friend Régine, or with her mother and sisters. But, despite public disapproval, her ambition persisted. Maman occasionally took her three beautiful daughters to the Alcazar, the most famous popular theatre in Marseilles. Their father never accompanied them on these excursions. For him, the word 'actress' was synonymous with 'whore', and he wished to see his daughters settled, possibly with sons of his business associates. The thought of one of them becoming part of the theatrical world horrified him.

When Gaby was in her teens, Hippolyte was in his fifties and, after working so hard for so long, he wanted a little peace. Bored with the constant entreaties and pleadings from both his wife and Gaby, he finally agreed, on the condition that she finish her formal education, that Gaby could enter the Conservatoire de Musique at Marseilles and learn to sing. Perhaps he had visions of her studies there leading to a comparatively respectable career as an opera singer. His tough attitude towards Gaby may also have been softened a little by the recent marriage of his eldest and favourite daughter, Aimée, to the son of Monsieur Fleury, an old family friend and well-to-do businessman. In October 1898 Gaby started her studies at the conservatoire. These studies took the form of three different courses: singing, diction, and scale singing, or *solfège*. She enjoyed herself tremendously, although she was not physically strong, and she missed many classes due to throat infections and chest colds, to which she seemed particularly prone.

In 1899, tragedy struck the Caire family again. Barely a year after her marriage, Aimée died, the second member of her family to fall victim to tuberculosis. Gaby's studies at the Conservatoire were temporarily halted as the family went into a period of mourning. She resumed her classes after approximately six months, but the interruption meant that the grades she achieved in her final examinations were mediocre. She was, nonetheless, awarded a first prize for *solfège* in the summer of 1901. Although her voice was not powerful by any means, she had at least learnt to sing in key. This was in itself insufficient to open the doors of the Opéra, or even the

4

Opéra Comique, but it was certainly a talent that would help her to get work in the music halls on which by now she had set her sights. And besides, her voice was secondary to something she possessed in abundance – personality, and the beginnings of her own unique style.

Today, many of the women of Marseilles display a love of show in the almost brash stylishness of their dress. The boulevards and side streets seem to be full of strutting beauties in impossibly high heels; very short, or indeed, very long skirts, brightly printed or in the vivid, clear hues of the current fashion; loaded with jewellery both real and fake; and exhibiting the kind of overblown chic that verges on vulgarity. They call it *l'exuberance Marseillaise*, and Gaby had it in abundance.

Of course, she was still very young, and had a great deal to learn about how to dress her hair and wear her clothes well. Make-up was unheard of – even actresses on stage wore comparatively little. The most a respectable girl could do to heighten her natural colour was to bite her lips and pinch her cheeks. Not that Gaby needed any artificial help. Her fair skin, golden-brown hair, startlingly expressive eyes and beautiful smile were sufficient to get her all the attention she needed. These looks, coupled with her slightly plump figure – as was fashionable at the time – her quick sense of humour and her dogged determination to succeed, were the weapons with which she set out to conquer the music hall.

After leaving the conservatoire, Gaby's next step was trying to find employment. To her father's intense displeasure, she began to look for work in the local theatres. She soon found that it was a hopeless task: she was just one pretty girl among many young hopefuls; perhaps a little prettier than most, but she had no experience, no dance training, nothing in fact to offer but her looks and enthusiasm. Doggedly persistent though she was, in her almost daily trek round the managers' offices, the answer to her request for work was always the same – no.

She began to despair of ever finding work in Marseilles. Home was not a happy place since Aimée's death. The family had moved yet again to a new house and shop, at 52, rue Tapis-Vert, then an elegant street near the Church of St Pius, but this did little to raise family spirits. Rows between Gaby and her father about her career became an almost daily occurrence. She had a volatile temper, but a deeply ingrained respect for her parents forced her to keep this in check, and she passed many an evening alone in her room, seething with impotent rage. She began planning her escape. Leaving home was a big step, but she began to realize that, if her ambitions were to be fulfilled, she would have to try her luck in Paris.

Paris at the turn of the century . . . What images that conjures up, even now. The intensity of the images it excited in the mind of a stage-struck provincial girl at the time is not hard to imagine. Gaby had heard of the Moulin Rouge and the Folies-Bergère, and although she had not yet set her sights so high, she knew that there were dozens of smaller halls, even cafés, that offered musical entertainment, and where she would be able to find work and gain experience. Never for one moment did she doubt that one day she would be a famous celebrity. Once, when she was still a convent schoolgirl, she had had her palm read by a gipsy at one of the annual local fairs, and the old woman had told her that her hand revealed great fame and fortune. She had excitedly repeated the prophecy over the dinner table that night. Her mother had smiled indulgently, but her father had glowered, and snapped that it was a sin for a Catholic girl to believe in such nonsense.

Alone in her room, she formulated plans for her new life. Firstly, she would need a new name. She thought of the actresses and singers she admired: Réjane, Yvette Guilbert, Polaire. The names rolled off the tongue, looked good on posters, and sounded romantic. Gabrielle Caire sounded too bourgeoise, and was too long. Stories abound about how she found her stage name. According to one version, her maternal grandparents were florists with a market stall in the Canebière, on which Gaby helped out on Saturdays. One day she was spotted there, surrounded by lilies, by a Parisian theatrical agent called Jules Binot. Binot was struck by her beauty, fell into conversation with her, discovered she wanted to be an actress, and suggested that she call herself 'Gabrielle of the Lilies'.

Charming though this explanation is, it seems too romantic to be true. It is more likely that the name Gaby Deslys evolved from her mother's pet name for her – Gaby-Elise. She was, however, undecided about her stage name at this point; the most important thing was making the move north.

Exact details of this move remain obscure. In every story ever printed about her, it is claimed she was romantically attached at the time: either to a young violinist called Peter Lepkovitch; a dancer called Pierre, who got her her first job; or, according to André Négis in his book *Parisians du Midi*, to a much older man who played Des Grieux to Gaby's Manon. This last is the classic story of an innocent young country girl who is taken off to the big city by an older man, and eventually comes to a bad end. It is hard to know what to believe. According to some sources, Gaby was involved even at this tender age with an even younger Sacha Guitry, son of one of France's greatest dramatic actors, Lucien Guitry, and eventually one of the best-known figures in French cinema and theatre. Whatever the truth of the matter, it is difficult to imagine a young girl at that time setting out alone to make her way in the metropolis. But she was already twenty-one, no longer a child. She was also extremely ambitious, and desperate to escape from the stifling atmosphere of home. She had the address of one of her teachers at the conservatoire, Marie-Thérèse Kolb, who had become a friend, and who had recently moved to Paris. Madame Kolb knew Gaby's parents, and she had promised to keep an eye on their daughter.

Although Gaby was glad to get away from her father, it was a wrench to leave Maman and her sister Matichon. There were tearful farewells at Gare St Charles on the autumn morning in 1902 that Gaby boarded the Paris Express.

2

NIGHT CLASSES

When Gaby arrived in Paris, the first thing she did was to contact Marie-Thérèse Kolb, who found her somewhere to live. It was also through Madame Kolb that Gaby got her first job, at the Parisiana, a small music hall on the boulevard de la Poissonière. Her name – simply 'Gaby' – appears in very small letters at the bottom of the programme of a revue called *Y a des Surprises*, which opened on 9 October 1902. When she saw how young the other girls in the chorus were, some already having two or three years' experience behind them, she felt a little old at twenty-one to be a raw beginner. So she took four years off her age, four years she was never to regain.

The work was pretty dull, but she was grateful for it. It consisted mostly of walking on and off stage and general chorus work. There was a great deal of dancing on the programme, and Gaby felt at a distinct disadvantage. She had had some tuition in singing, but none whatever in dance. She managed to bluff her way through most routines, but when the whole chorus got together for the quadrille or cancan, the standard finale in many halls in Paris by this time, she was at a loss. But she was willing to improve. She rehearsed long and hard, was never late, and always the last to leave. Every spare moment she had, she gave over to learning her craft. She became friendly with the dance captain and had extra classes. Although her wages were small, barely enough to live on, she always found enough money to visit as many other halls and theatres as possible, when she was not herself performing. She did not merely go to amuse herself, she regarded it as an education. She was the student, the big names on the stage were her tutors. She studied exactly what they did, as closely as an artist studies his model, trying to analyse exactly what made them great. She soon learned that they all had one quality in common, that elusive thing called personality: a charisma that was unique to them; a style that was always original, never copied. She watched how the great solo performers held and controlled their audiences as surely as a puppeteer pulls the strings of a marionette. She noticed how certain artists could do this even in places like the Folies-Bergère, where the performance taking place on the stage was merely incidental to the eating, drinking and soliciting taking place in the auditorium.

The Folies-Bergère gave Gaby her first glimpses of the *demi-monde*. Parisian society at the turn of the century could be roughly divided into two. On the one hand there was the respectable establishment or *monde*, its elegant salons presided over by wealthy and aristocratic hostesses. On the other hand there was the *demi-monde*, ruled by a handful of courtesans who had become notorious. Too grand and glamorous ever to be called prostitutes, they were variously known as *les dégrafées* (the unbuttoned ones); *cocottes*; or, more descriptively, *les agenouillées* (the kneelers); or *horizontales*. Their mansions, flashily modish clothes, and most of all their vast collections of gems, proclaimed that the wages of sin were excellent. Several of them pursued careers as 'actresses', and the three best known *grandes horizontales*, Caroline (*La Belle*) Otéro, Liane de Pougy, and Emilienne d'Alençon, were all stars of the music hall.

Otéro was probably the most famous, and the most talented theatrically. Colette, in her memoirs, describes Otéro's voice as being 'major in tone, true in pitch', but it was her erotic, abandoned dancing that formed a major part of this supposed Spanish gipsy's stage act. Much of her success was due to her reputation. Her tastes – which ran to a diamond corselet by Cartier so valuable that, when she produced it for special stage appearances, two armed guards watched over it from the wings, and custom-built Mercedes limousines – were such that she could only ever be the plaything of the very richest men. A great deal of her jewellery came from:*

'a hideous German baron called Ollstreder whom she'd
captured when she danced in Berlin. He was a horrible old
lecher who never confused love with love-making. There
was never any romantic courtship or subtle build-up to his

---

*Extract from *Elegant Wits and Grand Horizontals* by Cornelia Otis Skinner.

attentions. Any evening he wanted Caroline's services, he'd send her a box from Cartier's containing some costly item, and his calling card. "On such a basis," Otéro had told her maid, "one can't call a man ugly".'

Whichever stage she happened to be dancing on was Otéro's shop window. Although the majority of the audience could only afford to do what the French call 'lick the window', there was always the chance that a theatre box might contain a new baron who could afford to sample the goods.

Otéro's greatest rival for the title of 'world's most expensive whore' was, for a while, Liane de Pougy. Liane had been famous ever since she made her Paris debut at the Folies-Bergère, and had been wildly applauded by the Prince of Wales. It transpired that she had, with great and commendable effrontery, written him a note beforehand, saying, 'Sire, I am about to make my debut in Paris at the Folies-Bergère. I would be consecratedly yours if you would come and applaud me'. It is not known whether he took up this offer, but she became a celebrity overnight. It rapidly became known that the pretty young dancer 'with royal connections' could be had for a very high price, and soon Liane was in business, swapping her favours for furs, jewels, works of art and even houses.

She was never very talented on stage, although one or two of her set pieces had a certain shock value. She appeared, again at the Folies-Bergère, in a sketch called *L'Araignée d'Or*, dressed – almost – as a golden spider, her costume consisting of a few tatters of gold lace, in which she posed at the centre of a vast, shimmering wire web, in which were trapped several helpless male victims, all elegantly attired in full evening dress. The piece had been written for her by her great friend, the gossip columnist Jean Lorrain, who specialized in his own brand of outrageousness, not only with his scurrilous writing but also in his general appearance. A tall, burly figure with peroxide-blonde curled hair and full make-up, his daily public outings caused as much of a sensation as those of his friend Liane, who had once horse-whipped him in public after he wrote something unflattering about her in his column.

Great rivalry existed between Otéro and de Pougy, and there is a well-known story of an encounter between them at Maxim's. Otéro, knowing that de Pougy was expected there one night, determined to outshine her rival, and appeared wearing her entire collection of jewellery. Diamonds, rubies, pearls and sapphires flashed and glittered all over her body, from her ankles to her head. Her finery included ten huge ruby clips pinned to the plunging neckline of her dress, and necklaces that had belonged to the Empress Eugénie and the Empress of Austria. Just for good measure, the Cartier diamond corselet was firmly in place.

Liane, however, had been forewarned. She made her appearance late in the evening, clad in the simplest virginal white gown, devoid of any jewellery. A few paces behind came her maid, staggering under the weight of a cushion piled high with the glittering heap that constituted her mistress' collection of jewels. 'And all real', Liane was heard to remark loudly, knowing that Otéro's taste for anything that glittered often resulted in her wearing real gems and theatrical fakes indiscriminately.

The third leading *horizontale* was Emilienne d'Alençon, a voluptuous blue-eyed blonde, whose gentle, ladylike manner belied her mercenary nature. But although she was as ambitious as the other two, she had a softer personality, and a kind heart.

In common with de Pougy and Otéro, d'Alençon had made her debut at the Folies-Bergère, where she presented a novelty act with a troupe of tame rabbits that were dyed pink and wore paper ruffs. She had a long-lasting liaison with the aged and lecherous King Leopold of Belgium, and another with the youthful Duc d'Uzès. When the latter died of dysentery in Africa, his mother, the Duchess, discovered that a priceless family heirloom, an antique emerald necklace, was missing. Guessing accurately where it might be, the Duchess wrote to d'Alençon, who promptly returned it to her. In appreciation of d'Alençon's honesty, the Duchess sent her a magnificent solitaire diamond pendant. Despite her reputation as a *cocotte*, d'Alençon's many kindnesses included adopting the son of a prostitute friend, and taking him everywhere with her. When she wasn't conducting her well-publicized affairs, or teaching her pink rabbits new tricks, this surprising woman spent her spare time composing romantic poetry – a volume of which, entitled *Sous la Masque*, was published in 1915 – or studying the stock market.

Gaby was by turns fascinated and repelled by this world. Although slightly horrified by the implications of her discovery, she learnt very quickly that publicity, or notoriety, was the key to success: these famous *horizontales* did, after all, seem to have very little talent – on stage, at least. She saw how other, more legitimate, stars promoted themselves. A unique style of dressing was one way, though she could not see herself going as far as the celebrated Polaire, whose publicity gimmicks included combing her black hair into a wild frizz, painting her tongue a livid red, and piercing her nose with a large gold ring.

Gaby filed all this information in the back of her mind for future reference. In the meantime, the endless rehearsals and practice continued. Whatever talents she might have, she was determined to fully develop and exploit them. Through Marie-Thérèse Kolb, Gaby was introduced to a drama coach, Madame Paravicini, and lessons with her were added to an already hectic schedule. After several months' hard work, she felt confident enough to apply to the Mathurins Theatre, whose manager, Jules Berny, she had been told, was planning a new revue, and was looking for fresh faces. He was impressed enough by her youthful looks and personality to give her a job. Berny had a new song called *Je Chante la Gloire de la Parisienne*, and had been looking for someone to sing it. He thought it would be amusing to have the glories of Parisian womanhood extolled in Gaby's thick Marseilles accent.

One of Berny's friends was the young artist Jacques-Charles, later to become one of the period's greatest revue directors, and Gaby's close friend. He recalled the impression she made on him at their first meeting as follows:*

> 'She was quite short, with a rounded, bouncy figure, her calves imprisoned in high button boots. An adorable blonde doll, hair as curly as a six-month-old lamb, pink as a fondant, big blue eyes wide and surprised, and an adorable mouth no bigger than a strawberry.'

Berny's judgement was right, for the combination of Gaby's fresh looks, curvaceous figure, and an accent that the audience

*Extract from *De Gaby Deslys à Mistinguett* by Jacques-Charles.

thought hysterical, was a winner. From that day on, she was never out of work. The curly blonde wig that Berny made her wear became something of a fixture, until she dispensed with it entirely and started to lighten the natural blonde lights in her own hair. Her social life blossomed, but she did not let it interfere with her career. It was more important that her mornings were spent in dance class than in bed with a hangover. Not that she was averse to the occasional dinner at Maxim's after the show. Being seen in the most elegant restaurant in Paris was an important public relations exercise for any rising young actress.

Opened in May 1899, Maxim's had rapidly established a reputation as the headquarters of the international playboy set. Gallons of vintage champagne, kilos of Beluga caviare were consumed nightly and the rich of America, Brazil, even Russia, were helped in the rapid dissipation of their fortunes by the most glamorous members of the *demi-monde*. Under the indulgent eye of the manager, Cornuché, anything could happen – from La Belle Otéro dancing a wild fandango on her table, to Russian princes scattering handfuls of gold coins in the air. Theatrical personalities rubbed shoulders with the more louche members of French high society, and gossip columnists like Jean Lorrain made sure they were never too drunk to miss anything.

This was a glittering new world for Gaby, and despite her dedication to her work, she wanted to explore it. Because she was now a featured player, she received more invitations to dine at Maxim's than she could ever hope to accept. So she was very selective, only accepting after repeated requests, and then only from the kind of slim young man that she found attractive. On the rare occasions when she let a much older man take her out, she made it quite clear that, no matter what expensive gifts he gave her, she was no trainee *horizontale*, and the evening would not conclude in bed. This did not seem to deter the majority of the ageing Lotharios who came to see her show night after night, and who bombarded her dressing room with visiting cards and flowers. For most desired not sexual conquest, but prestige; just to be seen in the company of a very beautiful young girl at Maxim's was enough. Besides, there seemed to be no shortage of wealthy and attractive young men just as eager for her attentions. Gaby was shocked, however, to see some of the revolting old lechers other girls in the theatre were prepared to sleep with for financial gain. Although she was no prude, and indeed, by this time, certainly no virgin, she had no intention of prostituting herself in this way. She had rather girlish, romantic notions of love, and all that it entailed, and felt sure that one day the right man would come into her life, and that it would be forever. But she wasn't ready for that quite yet. Like any young girl new to the 'Big City', first she wanted to have a little fun. Her face gradually became known around town. She was often seen on the arm of a suitable young *beau*, but seldom with the same one twice. And although the mere fact that she was working in the music hall meant that she moved on the periphery of the *demi-monde*, no scandal was attached to her name in these early days. She was merely one of dozens of pretty, ambitious young starlets, trying to make a name for themselves in a competitive and overcrowded profession.

For her appearance at the Mathurins, and a subsequent one at the Marigny, Gaby was billed simply as Deslys. Still undecided about a stage name, she changed it totally for her next appearance, at the Scala. *M'zelle Chichi* opened there on 30 March 1904, and Gaby is listed on the programme under the name of Nhiska. She undoubtedly thought this sounded more exotic than either Gaby or Deslys. It was, however, a short-lived transformation, and this was the only occasion on which she used the name. Gaby's, or rather Nhiska's, character was called Nini Sommier, an ambitious *demi-mondaine* of a type that Gaby would often portray in the future.

This was the first of a couple of seasons at the Scala that would prove significant in Gaby's career. Nini Sommier was her most substantial rôle to date, and she found herself on the same bill as some famous music-hall stars including Jeanne Dirys, Aimée ('Miss') Campton, and the notorious Emilienne d'Alençon. Gaby was at first wary of this woman, about whom so much gossip abounded, but she was surprised to find her gentle and full of charm, in direct contrast to de Pougy and Otéro, whose aggressive bitchiness was as legendary as their diamonds. The two became friends, and, to a certain extent, d'Alençon took Gaby under her wing. It is even possible that she effected introductions between the pretty young actress and wealthy men of her acquaintance who she thought

14

would make suitable escorts. She certainly gave Gaby her advice, and the benefit of her years of experience in dealing with men. Gaby, always thirsty for knowledge, made an eager listener. She learned from d'Alençon that it was possible, if a woman was clever enough, to get a great deal out of life without sacrificing her self-respect. As for her reputation, 'Well,' said d'Alençon, 'it's a little late for me to think of that'.

Although Gaby had no intention of treading the same lurid path as the older woman, she felt that she could gain a great deal by listening to her. On discussing her life with d'Alençon, Gaby realized that she herself had a basic distrust of men that stemmed from her father's domination of her childhood. She realized also that one of the motivating forces behind her ambition was a determination never to be dominated or manipulated by anyone again. If there was any question of manipulation in a relationship, Gaby would be the one who pulled the strings.

Gaby's second Scala appearance was in the revue *A Fleur de Peau*, which opened in December 1904. Nhiska was no more; the name GABY DESLYS appeared in the programme in medium-sized type, some way below that of the star, Arlette d'Orgère. By now Gaby's personal style was beginning to evolve. The postcards printed as publicity for this show reveal, under a cockade of curls and ostrich feathers, the confident yet shy smile of a still very young girl, dressed, it appears, in her first really grown-up gown, all spangles, ruffles, and low *décolleté*. She seems a little plump by modern standards, but her ample bosom and nipped-in waist conform perfectly with the ideals of feminine beauty prevalent at the time. She had also, evidently, made her first important conquest, for a fine row of pearls glistens around her neck – the precursor of many.

She was very good on stage, both to look at and to listen to. Her voice, though not strong, was pleasant, and good enough for her to put across the funny, satirical songs that were a feature of Parisian revues at the time. These revues, of which *A Fleur de Peau* was typical, really did review something, unlike their American and British counterparts. All the current gossip of the boulevards was introduced, and although Gaby was no great emotive singer in the mode of Yvette Guilbert, she had natural comic timing, which, combined with her looks, proved irresistible. Before long, she was making enough money to rent a comfortable flat on rue Constantinople. Coming as she did from a family of merchants, she was very shrewd financially, and she managed to save a percentage of her wages every week.

In common with many other young actresses, Gaby acted as a mannequin for one or two fashion houses. This merely involved being seen in the smartest places, wearing clothes from the newest collections. It was a convenient way for her to look wonderful without spending a single franc. When the theatres closed for the long summer break, and society migrated to the coast, the mannequins went with them at the couturiers' expense. Thus Gaby enjoyed a few weeks in Monte Carlo, and became a great success at the casino, where pretty girls and members of the *demi-monde* were always in demand as 'mascots'. Millions of francs were won and lost nightly at the tables, and a wealthy gambler on a lucky streak would always reward his mascot with the odd thousand-franc chip, or a little something from Cartier. Never a gambler, Gaby cashed in all the chips that came her way and, judging from the jewellery she wore on stage the following winter, the little somethings from Cartier were many.

Back in Paris, her mother and sister Matichon came up from Marseilles and joined her in rue Constantinople. Gaby already knew from her mother's letters that her parents' marriage had been foundering for some time. Their rows had been frequent, and often about the same thing – Gaby. Monsieur Caire's attitude towards his daughter's chosen career had not changed, and he blamed his wife for encouraging her to pursue it. His only other surviving daughter, Matichon, was now contemplating the same career path, and was also receiving her mother's encouragement. This had proved too much for the old man, and there had been one or two very violent rows. His wife claimed that his character had undergone a complete transformation since Aimée had died and Gaby had left home: he had become irascible, and prone to deep depressions followed by violent outbreaks of temper. Madame Caire, after years of being dominated by her husband, had had enough.

When she and Matichon arrived in Paris, they found Gaby much changed by her brief stay there. They were amazed at how she had matured, how well she had done in a little over two years. Maman saw, however, that the blonde sophistication of her daughter was only skin-deep; soon the two sisters were laughing and giggling like schoolgirls. Gaby was delighted that her sister was considering a stage career, and promised that she would try to find work for her. She later confessed privately to Matichon that she had had one or two lovers, but no one she cared about, no one serious. Matichon's eyes opened wide when Gaby showed her the beautiful clothes she had acquired at no expense, and her growing collection of jewellery. 'It's easy,' Gaby assured her, 'This whole city is full of rich, generous men. If you play your cards right, they'll give you anything. You don't even have to sleep with them,' she giggled, relishing her sister's shocked expression, '. . . unless you want to.'

Madame Caire and Matichon were in Paris to witness Gaby's rapid rise to fame. She landed a plum job at the Olympia Theatre, the Commère, in a revue written by Victor de Cottens, called *Au Music Hall*, which opened on 10 May 1905. It was a successful show. Gaby introduced a wide variety of acts, starting with a film show and ending with a human cannonball. She also sang one or two risqué little songs. She was clad throughout in the typical *soubrette*'s uniform, consisting of a big hat trimmed with ostrich feathers, a short, low-cut dress with full skirts and dozens of lacy petticoats, silk stockings, fancy garters, and high-buttoned boots. It was her biggest part to date, and the first one that really brought her into the public eye. Just one month after the revue opened, she was on the cover of the popular weekly magazine *Paris Qui Chante*, and a minor celebrity.

3

GAIETY GIRL

One night, the audience at the Olympia included the celebrated actor, George Grossmith Junior. Grossmith had long been associated with George Edwardes and his world-famous Gaiety Theatre in London. One of the things the Gaiety was famous for was the extravagant 'prettiness' of all the musical comedies produced there, and every night all sections of society crammed the impressive neo-classical building which stood at the corner of The Strand and Aldwych. The chorus was supposed to be the loveliest in the world; for any aspiring showgirl, working at the Gaiety was a sure sign of having arrived, in a theatrical sense. In addition, many members of the chorus subsequently married into the aristocracy. In Gaby's day, for example, Zena Dare married the Hon. Maurice Brett; Mabel Russell married Cecil Rhodes' nephew, Stanley; Sylvia Storey became Countess Poulett . . . The list could go on and on. This link between the Gaiety and the peerage was well-documented by the press, and as a result all the chorus girls in London were practically climbing over each other to work there.

As well as acting in various Gaiety Theatre productions, George Grossmith partly wrote and produced several. His associate, George Edwardes, general manager of the Gaiety, was one of the most famous British men of the theatre of the pre-First World War years. A big, handsome Irishman, by this time in his fifties, he had specific ideas about the kind of girls he wanted for his productions, and George Grossmith knew them exactly. Most weekends, when the curtain came down on Saturday night, George Grossmith would catch the night train and ferry to Paris, spend Sunday there, and leave in enough time to appear on stage at the Gaiety on Monday night. During one of these weekends, he found himself watching the show at the Olympia, when a petite, shapely blonde came on stage, and in a small, clear, light operatic voice sang a rather saucy song.

Grossmith knew that in the show Edwardes was planning for the coming winter season, an up-to-date musical comedy version of *Aladdin*, there was a part for a young French girl to play the princess' French maid. Most of the play was cast, but they still needed this one actress. Grossmith thought Gaby fitted the bill very nicely. He knew that George Edwardes had a penchant for blondes, and on his return to London persuaded the impresario to accompany him to Paris the next weekend. George Edwardes took one look at Gaby and told Grossmith she was far too glamorous to be anyone's maid, but that he had to have her for the show. Maybe they could write in a new part better suited to her physical charms.

It wasn't too difficult to persuade Gaby to visit England. Largely due to the great popularity in Paris of the Prince of Wales, subsequently King Edward VII, all things British had acquired a kind of chic; many English words and phrases found their way into the French language at this time. When fashion-conscious Parisians were not enjoying their 'fif' o'clock' tea and 'sandwiches', they were possibly planning 'le weekend' in London, where they might stock up with tailored tweeds and Scotch. Whilst the *entente cordiale* was in full swing, French entertainers were always happy to be offered the chance to cross the Channel. Gaby's contract would be for three months from September of 1906, and in his fluent French, Grossmith negotiated a contract with Gaby that would allow her a considerable weekly amount as a living allowance, as well as providing comfortable quarters for her at the Carlton Hotel. He told her that *The New Aladdin* would be the most lavish production ever staged at the Gaiety, and promised that her costumes would be decorative in the extreme. They had even written in a new part for her – 'The Charm of Paris'. She would not even have to speak any English, which was just as well, for her knowledge of the language was minimal.

Leaving Maman behind in Paris, she arrived in London in August. Rehearsals began almost immediately. The show was fraught with difficulties from the start, the main one being that the leading lady, Gertie Millar, could not join it as planned because her husband, Lionel Monckton, was seriously ill. Even worse, Monckton had been contracted to write a large part of the musical score, including Gertie's numbers, and was too ill to do so. Lily Elsie was brought in to take Gertie's part but, charming though she was, Gertie was a star and she was not. These difficulties upset George Edwardes who had ambitious plans for *Aladdin*. He was a little tired of the format of musical comedy at the Gaiety, and *Aladdin* was planned on much more ambitious lines, and billed as 'A Musical Extravaganza'. One of the gimmicks he added involved Gaby wrestling with a Japanese judo expert whilst singing 'The Ju Jitsu Waltz'. Her partner was a tiny Japanese called Yukio-Tani. Smaller even than Gaby herself, he was one of the world's greatest exponents of his art. One day Edwardes was watching Gaby and Tani practice, and was fascinated at the ease with which Tani flicked her up into the air, always making sure that she landed on her feet.

'How on earth do you do it?' Edwardes asked.

'Come, I show you,' said Tani.

Edwardes was a big man, weighing at least sixteen stone, and it seemed unlikely that the tiny Tani would even be able to lift him. Tani, however, took Edwardes' hand and flicked him up in the air as easily as he had Gaby, landing the astonished Irishman on his feet. Everyone was shocked, Edwardes was astonished.

'How on earth do you do it?' he repeated. Once more the tiny Japanese grabbed his hand and whirled him through the air. This time, however, he did not land so well, bumping roughly down on his back. Everyone rushed forward to help him up. He soon recovered, but snapped furiously at Tani, 'Don't ever do that again, I'm much too old for that sort of thing'. In the future, Edwardes steered well clear of his oriental star.

On the opening night after the first few scenes, it became obvious that something was wrong with the show. The audience were restive, and Gaby's scenes were the only ones that drew any real applause. She had a sensational first entrance: Aladdin rubbed his magic lamp, and wished for 'all the charm of Paris'. From a huge basket of silk roses, wearing an outfit almost identical to the one George Grossmith had first seen her in at the Olympia, Gaby burst out. At the sight of this vision in low-cut dress, ruffled petticoats, beribboned garters, and high-buttoned boots, the audience exploded into spontaneous applause. Her next appearance provoked a similar reaction. With the vulnerable, innocent sexiness of an Edwardian Marilyn Monroe, she sang a very silly song called 'Sur la Plage'. The opening lyric, 'When I take my *bain de mer*, at what do the men all stare?, drew wild applause from the men in the audience, as it was obvious what anyone would stare at. From the auditorium, the bathing dress she was wearing appeared to be slashed almost to the waist, her modesty protected by the two glittering starfish that perched on her breasts. As she continued the song, her small voice could hardly be heard above the whoops and wolf whistles. It provided the sensation of the evening. After she left the stage, the audience soon became bored again, and many of them talked loudly through the second act. The curtain fell to polite applause, and a few jeers from the balcony.

Gaby came forward to take her bow, feeling confused and unhappy, worried that the audience's displeasure with the show extended to her. She need not have worried. When she curtseyed at the footlights, the jeers miraculously changed to wolf whistles and cheers. When she realized that every man in the audience was on his feet, wildly applauding, she felt a profound sense of relief.

The reviews for *Aladdin* were terrible, but without exception they mentioned Gaby Deslys as being one of the best things in it. Even *The Times* called her 'alluring'. She was a star overnight. She was photographed, interviewed, fêted wherever she went. The *Tatler* and the *Sketch* both carried full-page pictures of her in her daring bathing costume. The former published a long article, 'London as seen by a Parisian actress', in which she said all the right things about 'your beautiful foggy city, wonderful policemen', etcetera. And Pears Soap commissioned her to endorse their product. Fame came to Gaby like a fabulous new jewel – one she was happy to wear constantly.

On two occasions, the show was interrupted by admirers who got carried away. One night, as she came on stage, an elderly gentleman sitting in the front row of the stalls leapt up. Shouting out how much he loved her, he threw his gold watch and chain, his cigarette case and all his money onto the stage at her feet. He was seized and escorted off the premises, Gaby making sure he got his property back. She was intensely embarrassed by the incident; the old man was obviously deranged, but nevertheless it started tongues wagging. A few weeks later, she had to defend herself when an elderly and very drunken pillar of the aristocracy managed to climb on stage halfway through her opening number, and made a grab for her. Before other members of the cast came to her rescue and dragged him away, she had to fight him off. No doubt some of the audience found these incidents shocking, wondering what sort of woman could excite men to this sort of behaviour.

By day, Gaby worked constantly to improve her performance. She had private dance tuition from Will Bishop, one of the best choreographers in London, as well as lessons in singing and in English. At Christmas her contract was finished, but, conscious of her value to the show, she asked for, and got, a large salary increase. Gertie Millar finally joined the show, as did Lionel Monckton's new numbers, and following this injection of talent, *Aladdin* managed to run for an additional three months. Later in the year, George Edwardes announced to the board of directors, on the stage of the Gaiety, that the show had lost money, partly because it had cost a phenomenal £30,000 to mount, but mainly because it had just not appealed to popular taste.

Aladdin had been a financial disaster – but it had been the making of Gaby Deslys. Carrying with her a contract to appear the following winter season at the Alhambra, she returned to Paris in the spring of 1907.

Gaby had no delusions about herself: she was well aware of her potential, and also of her limitations. She knew that, if she was going to achieve her ambition of international celebrity, and the wealth that would accompany it, she would have to work very hard. She had done well enough for a girl in her mid-twenties, especially well when one considers that she had had a formal education, and had not been able to start her working life until she was twenty-one. However, she had not yet topped any bill. Her sheer professionalism kept her in work: although no singer, she could memorize a song after hearing it once or twice. The same principle applied to her dancing: though fairly gifted, she was no Pavlova. Still, the most complicated choreography was not beyond her, and she worked hard to master every routine quickly.

She had found the perfect dance teacher in Will Bishop. His long and distinguished career had started with the Empire Ballet in 1893, and he had spent many seasons dancing and producing dance at the Empire, as well as the Gaiety, and at George Edwardes' other theatre, Daly's. He was introduced to Gaby soon after she arrived in London, and he arranged the little dances she did in *The New Aladdin*. He was amazed at her total professionalism and said in an interview many years later:

'I was as fit as a boxer who had trained to the last ounce when Gaby began taking lessons with me, but she used to dance me off my feet at rehearsals. After an hour I used to suggest that she might like a rest, as she must be tired. But no, she wasn't. "No, I must go on, I must get it exactly right before I stop."

'I never met anyone so indefatigable or persevering in my whole life. When she was learning a new dance *nothing* else mattered. She simply lived for it. Not once, but on several occasions after she went back to Paris and was preparing for a new show, she used to arrange to get down to the theatre at ten o'clock in the morning, and no matter what time she went to bed at night she was always there on time.

'All her letters to me, and she wrote many in the years following her engagement at the Gaiety, were about dancing.'

Gaby learnt to trust Will Bishop implicitly. For two or three years she had him arrange all her dances, often paying him to travel long distances to do so. It was well worth her while. The Gaiety engagement was one of her few excursions into the legitimate theatre, as opposed to the music hall, and a vast chasm separated these two worlds. Music-hall artists were responsible for arranging their own acts, and it was on the strength of this that they succeeded or failed. Because they were on stage for just a few minutes – only the biggest names would appear for longer, at most half an hour – variety artists had to make an unusually powerful and immediate impact with material, costumes, music, choreography, and all the other weapons in their armoury. Gaby realized that her appearance was the thing that would get her the most attention, and from very early in her career she made sure that she looked as ravishing as possible. She also made sure that her few minutes on stage were not marred by lack of rehearsal: she had to be perfect. The audience must never be disappointed, there was too much competition around for that.

The variety stages of both London and Paris were crowded with beautiful girls, and an incredibly varied and talented array of

23

performers. To succeed, you had to be good. Gaby knew from the start that she didn't have the voice of either Yvette Guilbert or Marie Lloyd, but in the looks department she had them both well and truly beaten. Guilbert was not as gaunt and haggard as Toulouse Lautrec had portrayed her, but she was no beauty. And, despite her enormous talent, if Marie Lloyd were to succeed in show business today, she would have to have her teeth fixed.

Of course, they were not all so plain. Some of the big stars of the time were truly beautiful, like Cléo de Mérode. She was a gifted dancer, but it was her flawless skin, heart-shaped face and perfect features, together with many rumours about her private life, that kept her in the public eye for years. Her unique way of dressing her hair, pulling it low over her ears into a chignon from a central parting, was universally copied, and became known as *le style Cléo*. Another great beauty, with talent to match, was Anna Held. Well-known in London and Paris, she was spotted by the American impresario Florenz Ziegfeld, who took her back to America as his bride, later to star her in his famous 'Follies'. Other, less talented, beauties were not so lucky. Their looks made an initial impact, but without the talent to back them up, they soon faded into obscurity.

Gaby quickly learnt that talent alone was enough to get you to the top of the bill, and keep you there, but looks alone were not. Her career was plotted and planned, step by step, and although fate was kind, when opportunities were revealed, she grabbed them with both hands, and made the very most of them.

4

APPLAUSE AND
CHAMPAGNE

Gaby had returned to Paris in 1907 a richer and wiser woman. The first thing she and Maman did was to go house-hunting. They both fell in love with a beautiful small villa a stone's throw from the Bois de Boulogne at 3, rue Henri-de-Bornier, built only a few years before with flowing Art-Nouveau decoration. The house was also conveniently situated for the Champs Elysées, where Gaby had signed for a season at Les Ambassadeurs, one of the smartest night spots in Paris. Although she had saved a lot, the purchase price of 160,000 francs at first seemed prohibitive. However, the amount was soon made up by the sale of a diamond and emerald necklace one of the grateful gamblers in Monte Carlo had given her a couple of years earlier. Loath though she was to part with any of her jewellery, she was very superstitious of the colour green, besides which she considered diamonds a little vulgar, and had developed a taste for the more subtle sheen of pearls.

Gaby's success in London had not gone unnoticed in Paris. On her return, she had been besieged with offers. She had accepted the engagement at Les Ambassadeurs because it enabled her to appear with Max Déarly, one of the most talented figures on the French variety stage. He was a brilliant comedian, a small, mobile-featured Parisian, who for several years had been the toast of the city. He sang rude songs with a deadpan expression, was a gifted acrobatic dancer, and a mimic. Gaby thought he would be a perfect foil for her fragile, apparently 'innocent' stage character, and she was right.

As soon as the contract was signed, she wrote to Will Bishop: 'I understand the revue will be put on about the 28 May, and I should therefore be very much obliged if you could come to Paris quickly as I want to rehearse. I am anxious we should give a pretty dance, and am counting on you to find something good.' She also managed to secure a place in the revue for a young English dancer called Vera Barton, the only member of the cast of *Aladdin* with whom she had become firm friends.

Though second on the bill to Déarly, Gaby's performance was well received, and the experience of working with one of the top comedians in France did much for her career. Déarly's performance was hysterical. One of the many impressions he did was of an English Tiller Girl dancing, cleverly observed and perfect in every detail – from the little side kick, to the ogle and smile at the Royal box as he went off. Gaby watched and noted every nuance of his performance, ever eager to pick up tips that she herself might use. His brilliant timing impressed her, and his close rapport with the audience was something she knew she had to try to develop: she had to get them on her side, appeal to their sympathy, as well as to their sense of humour and carnal desires.

The sympathy of her fellow performers was something that Gaby was also learning to cultivate and value. She became close, not necessarily to the stars, but to the chorus and orchestra, as well as the stage managers and dressers. Difficult and demanding though she may have been considered by management when negotiating contracts, especially as her status increased, she was always popular, indeed loved, by everybody backstage. She realised that only with the help of the technicians and chorus could she give a good performance, and she assiduously cultivated their friendship. She rightly deduced that, with the audience and the rest of the cast on your side, you could not go wrong.

The summer of 1907 passed quickly. Besides the successful revue at Les Ambassadeurs, decorating and furnishing the house at rue Henri-de-Bornier proved a time-consuming as well as expensive activity. Gaby had little time for romance. The parade of her admirers did not get any smaller as she became more famous, but she managed to stay unattached. She was truly 'wedded to her art'. If she had lovers, as she almost certainly did, the affairs must have been conducted very discreetly. She did, after all, share a home with her mother and sister. Her name appeared more frequently in the gossip columns, but as 'one of the loveliest actresses in Paris'. The name of Gaby Deslys was, as yet, untarnished by scandal.

She worked herself too hard. Consequently her health was variable. Her voice needed careful attention, as she had recurrent sore throats and chest colds. She never smoked cigarettes, even though it was considered fashionable, and the most she ever drank was the occasional glass of champagne, or a little Crème de Cacao after dinner.

Autumn came, and Gaby returned to London for the first of many successful seasons at the Alhambra. Under the directorship of Alfred Moul, the Alhambra had become one of a handful of music halls in London with a worldwide reputation. A vast and magnificent Moorish building in Leicester Square, it had had a chequered career. Originally opened as 'The Royal Panopticon of Science and Art' in 1854, for the first few years of its life it had been both a circus and a music hall, until it burned down in 1882, and was re-opened the following year as 'a showplace for comic opera and revue'. It had been the model for the Folies-Bergère, and had established a similiar reputation, not only in the acts it presented but also in its notoriety as a haunt both of the pleasure-loving aristocracy under the reign and patronage of King Edward VII, and of the working classes – as well as all the more expensive tarts in the West End.

Like an enormous Oriental palace, the Alhambra dominated Leicester Square, its hundreds of multi-coloured lights glimmering through the London fog, casting brilliant shadows on the motley crowds that nightly thronged the pavements outside. Although the sixpenny benches in 'the gods' were not comfortable, the boxes costing four guineas certainly were, and the medium-priced seating in the stalls and balconies had a reputation for being the most commodious in London. Alfred Moul was particularly fond of French actresses and singers, and many continental acts made their first appearance under the vast, twinkling mosque lights of his hall. Many people consider that, despite its then shabby condition, the destruction of the Alhambra to make way for a cinema, in the late 1930s, can be regarded as one of the biggest achitectural sins of the century.

In the winter of 1907 Gaby Deslys appeared in this theatre for the first time. She was on the same bill as a new rendition of the popular French operetta, *Les Cloches de Corneville*. Her fifteen-minute spot required her to play 'Diabolo'★ in a tightly-fitting sheath, which covered her from neck to ankles rather like a glamorous Egyptian mummy. During the course of the act, this slowly unwound to reveal a beaded, low-cut bathing dress, not unlike the one she had worn in *Aladdin*. This modified striptease caused a minor sensation, and was a theme she would develop in later years.

She varied this turn with one called '*La Journée d'une Parisienne,*' a saucy little song and dance choreographed by Will Bishop. Gaby loved her British audience. In Paris she was popular enough, but in London French actresses were considered something very special, particularly sexy and scintillating, and she was very rapidly learning to exploit this. Although her English was rapidly improving, she intentionally kept her French accent heavy; as a Marseillaise it amused and delighted her to be thought of as the very soul of Paris. She made it a rule never to discuss her background. If they wanted a Parisienne, she would wear a model of the Eiffel Tower on her head if necessary, and one day she would come close to even that.

Christmas came and went. Maman, who had stayed behind in Paris to supervise the furnishing and decorating of the new house, came over and helped her to get ready for her journey to Paris when her contract expired on 4 January 1908.

Alfred Moul was very eager to book her for the coming season, and although Gaby was willing to return to London, she was reluctant to commit herself just yet. She needed time to rest, to enjoy her new house and to see what offers might come up for the summer season in Paris – or elsewhere. She was eager to spread her wings, to travel more widely. Her success in London had made her feel she might repeat it elsewhere. The whole of Europe had variety houses eager to book sexy French acts: Vienna, Berlin, Budapest . . . She felt the world was her oyster. But her ultimate ambitions lay even futher afield, for the British papers were full of the huge salaries Marie Lloyd had commanded on her trip to America that year. Gaby would bide her time.

Back in Paris, she had little time to rest. She seemed driven by a ceaseless energy. Her mother, whilst delighted by her success,

★ The latest craze: a game involving balancing a double spinning top on a tautly held skipping rope.

would have liked her daughter to rest for a while. But fame was like a drug to Gaby; she was well and truly hooked. Her plans for foreign travel were temporarily shelved when she received an offer to play the Moulin Rouge for a short season that summer, at the top of the bill. Her partner would be Fred Wright, a charming, urbane English entertainer whose acquaintance she had made in London. Maman's protestations were in vain. Gaby promised that the contract would be for a few weeks only, and that afterwards they would take a real holiday. The faithful Will Bishop was summoned from London, and the rehearsals, singing lessons and costume fittings began all over again.

The title of the revue, *Son Altesse l'Amour* – His Highness, Love – would prove oddly prophetic.

Gaby was finally top of the bill. She had worked for six years, achieved fame to a degree, and was comfortably off with a nice house in Paris; she had a wardrobe of clothes that belonged to her, not to the dressmaker, and a trunk full of jewels. Doubtless she could go on working for a few years, but she knew she did not have the fabulous talent that could keep a star like Bernhardt or Réjane going well into middle age and beyond. She lived in dread of being old and poor. Someone had once told her the pathetic story of the miserable last days of an actress who was once the toast of Paris; how the actress who had been fêted and entertained, and who once lived, in Gaby's words on 'applause and champagne', had died in a miserable hovel. Her savings were inadequate, for she had spent freely, and the little she had left soon disappeared. In the end she had to beg for a crust of bread. She was forgotten by most of her friends of former days, and ignored by all. The terrible spectre of the poor old hag who had once been beautiful and successful haunted Gaby. Her fear of such an end increased her career drive. But if she was to achieve the great celebrity that would save her from a lonely, impoverished old age, something major had to happen.

On holiday in Cabourg that summer, after her brief but arduous season at the Moulin Rouge, Gaby lay in the shade of a large umbrella finalizing the details of her winter tour, and racking her brains as to what she could possibly do to make the whole world sit up and take notice.

5
THE MOST TALKED ABOUT WOMAN IN THE WORLD

Gaby returned to the Alhambra in March 1910 with a new sketch called *Les Caprices de Suzette*. It opened on 28 March to a packed house. Fans of Gaby's who remembered her from *The New Aladdin* were in for a surprise. She had changed.

The twenty-five-minute playlet opened with Gaby, a poor flower girl, looking for love, fame and fortune. But the poverty was soon dispensed with. After a short time Gaby reappeared, tricked up like an odalisque, loaded with pearls, lounging on vast silk cushions – an opulent, beguiling siren. The men in the audience were on the edge of their seats. Her tawny blonde hair was cut into a full, fluffy bob, echoing the many frothy, lace underskirts of her second outfit – a very short dress, more of a tutu really, but no ballerina ever looked like this. The leotard top had thin shoulder straps, its fine beaded fabric, shaded darker across the nipples, hardly restraining the prominent breasts beneath.

It was a startling transformation. When the spotlights hit her, perched on a high stool in this outfit, the gasps of the audience were audible. The naiveté that had captured audiences in *Aladdin* had only been a veneer; the sexy, self-assured star who warbled, high-kicked and strutted her way across the vast Alhambra stage was a totally different Gaby. Even those who had seen her in her revue at the Moulin Rouge just eighteen months earlier could hardly believe their eyes. What could possibly have happened in such a short time to so drastically alter her stage persona? She had always been pretty, but now the beauty of Gabrielle of the Lilies had extra lustre, as though finally gilded. Her eyes were as wide and expressive as ever, but now, when she smiled, as she did most of the time, it was in a provocative, slightly mocking way. She looked as if she knew something that you did not.

The preceding year had certainly been a busy one. Her old friend Will Bishop had taken a job at the Metropol in Berlin as dance director, and at his suggestion Gaby had gone there for a short season. One night the Crown Prince Wilhelm of Germany, otherwise known as Little Willie, had watched her performance, and had invited her to dine at the Adlon Hotel with one or two of his friends, including the Counts von Richter and Eulenberg. Willie had a reputation as a womaniser and a drunkard with a particular liking for sexy actresses, and although the incident was edifying in Gaby's career as a professional beauty, she could not have felt at ease in his company. Much was made of their meeting in the European press. One article suggested that he had fallen wildly in love with her, and that as a means of persuading her to break off the relationship, the Prince's father, Kaiser Wilhelm, had given her three black pearls, said to be the largest in the world.

Gaby, long having learnt the value of such publicity, made no comment. It was the first time her name had been mentioned in connection with royalty, and it gave her a new and delightful rôle to play – that of the courtesan. She thought of all the other actresses whose names had gone down in history because of real or imagined liaisons with kings and princes, from Nell Gwynn to Lola Montez. Even some of her contemporaries had done well on the strength of such exalted connections. From her very real relationship with the Prince of Wales, the beautiful but talentless Lillie Langtry had become a household name. The ravishingly beautiful Cléo de Mérode had become a star after King Leopold of Belgium had patted her head in a paternal way when she was presented to him after a performance. Even if they did have one or two meetings afterwards, Cléo had let it be known to all her close friends that the kind old man treated her like a daughter, and had never laid a finger on her. But that was not what the world thought. In Belgium, they even dubbed their elderly monarch 'Cleopold'. Meanwhile, whenever the dancer made an appearance, a curious public paid good money to see the 'notorious courtesan'. She eventually became a prima ballerina at the Paris Opéra.

31

Gaby was delighted to be associated with the Prince. Then, as she proceeded with her act from Berlin to Vienna to Budapest, the stories about her rumoured affairs got wilder. Her name was linked with that of Ferdinand of Bulgaria, and those of assorted dukes and princes of every realm from Luxembourg back to Leopold of Belgium himself. She derived great pleasure from reading about herself in the international gossip columns. 'Let's see where I am to be queen of this week,' she had joked to Maman, back in Paris in the late spring of 1909.

It had been an exhausting tour, but she loved working, and it had been worth it. She had been asking ever higher fees to appear, and theatre managements, more than willing to cash in on the publicity that now surrounded her, had been happy to pay. She had had numerous rich boyfriends, but nobody who meant anything to her. In the way of such things, as she became increasingly selective, the selection of men she had to choose from increased. Now, with her, albeit fictional, reputation as the plaything of kings, wealthy men wished to be seen in her company as the endorsement of their own success. She had never been more beautiful. Still only twenty-eight years old, she looked no more than the twenty-four she admitted to. By the summer of 1909, she was one of the most fashionable figures in Paris.

Gaby was always to be seen in the best places, at Longchamps for the races, dining at Maxim's; her clothes, her matchless jewels, her parties, filled the gossip columns day after day. Her clothes in particular gave the columnists plenty to write about. The fashion of the day required women to wear the largest hats ever known. Vast cartwheels of feathers, flowers, fruit and veiling were balanced on top of piled-up hair, and firmly skewered into place with lethal hatpins. Gaby had first worn one of these monsters on stage to great effect when she had played the part of a cockney coster girl with Fred Wright, a couple of years earlier at the Moulin Rouge. She had made the style her own. From then on, large hats featured heavily in all her stage costumes; the bigger and more outlandish they were, the more her public seemed to like them, and she didn't restrict their use to stage appearances. Photographs show her at the races, or just shopping on the Champs Elysées, her small, smiling face overshadowed by vast masterpieces of the milliners' art. The beautiful tail feathers of exotic birds were the most sought-after decorations; those taken from birds of paradise and egrets were the most desirable. Several rare species were decimated for the sake of fashion, and rare feathers became more costly than diamonds. Some of Gaby's hats cost hundreds of pounds, but on her last visit to London she had joined forces with the largest milliner there, Maison Lewis; and in return for publicizing their name, she had the pick of their enormous range.

She continued to wear huge, extravagant hats long after they went out of fashion, and they became her personal signature. She was also the innovator of the towering feathered headdresses that became an integral part of the spectacular revue in the form that reached its zenith in the 1920s, and which still exists today. In the 1960s, Gaby's hats gave Cecil Beaton inspiration for many of his designs for the film version of *My Fair Lady*. The now-famous Ascot scene features many identifiable 'Gaby' styles.★

For her next revue, not only were the hats sensational, but the costumes themselves were of breathtaking beauty. It was an extremely distinguished production which Gaby had chosen with great care from the many that were offered her. Staged at the Capucines, this production, entitled *Sans Rancune* (No Hard Feelings), was, in the luxury and extravagance of its costumes and sets, a landmark in the history of the spectacular revue. Written by P. L. Flers and Georges Thenon (better known as 'Rip'), it was a fast-moving, good-looking, very risqué production, built around Gaby Deslys in a series of amusing and visually delightful sketches and tableaux. One of the parts Gaby played was that of the demi-vierge (half-virgin) for which she appeared clad almost competely in rope after rope of shimmering pearls. No one doubted they were real. In another tableau, photographs of the time show her posed with Annie Perrey, a striking dark-haired foil to Gaby's blonde-ness, in a Russian snow scene, complete with horse-drawn sleigh. Both women are richly muffled in white arctic fox fur. Gaby sang, danced and told some outrageous jokes written for her by Rip,

★From *Cecil Beaton* by Hugo Vickers:
Cecil thought very carefully about each of the stars he dressed. (George) Cukor wanted Audrey Hepburn to look clean, slightly comic, but not chic . . . so Cecil at once turned to Gaby Deslys for inspiration.

which were calculated to make the best use of her still-persistent, if modified, Marseilles accent.

The whole of Paris was in love with her; her smiling face beamed down from hoardings twenty feet high from Montmartre to the Champs Elysées. Society flocked every night to the Capucines. Critics were delirious, not only about Gaby, but about all the supporting players, especially Spinelly, a dark elfin-faced comedienne and dancer, whose merciless send-up of Isadora Duncan and her 'aesthetic' dancing was one of the many hits of the programme. Week after week, business boomed. Winter approached, and nightly they played to packed houses. One night in late November, as Gaby sat in the star dressing room getting ready to go on, she can have had no idea that this was to be the most important performance of her career, and the night that would change her life.

Seated in a stage box was an extremely young and distinguished visitor, whose brief yet tragic life had captured the sympathy and imagination of the whole world – King Manuel of Portugal. He had succeeded to the throne a couple of years earlier, at the tender age of eighteen, under horrifically violent circumstances. On 1 February 1908, the whole Portuguese Royal Family, King Carlos, Queen Amelie and their two sons, were returning from a state occasion in an open carriage, when a group of Republican revolutionaries attacked them almost at the gates of the Royal Palace in Lisbon. At close range, they shot the King and the Crown Prince, killing the Crown Prince instantly, and mortally wounding the King. Indelibly engraved on young Manuel's mind forever was the image of his mother, standing up in the carriage, endeavouring to strike down with a great bouquet of roses, the rifle of one of the assassins before they escaped in the ensuing chaos. They left her cradling the head of her dying husband in her arms; his blood, and that of her dead son, covering her hands, splattered on her face, leaving great darkening stains on her blue silk dress.

Manuel had never expected to become King, had not been educated for the throne, and wore the crown of his troubled country unsteadily. Yet, in the brief period since the assassination, he had impressed everybody with his dignity and intelligence. His mother, a woman of tremendous strength and royal bearing (and the daughter of the Comte de Paris, pretender to the French throne), had done her utmost to assist her son in maintaining power in a country that was hopelessly divided politically, and on the verge of economic collapse. It was a difficult, if not impossible task, and the poor woman lived in terror lest her remaining son should share the fate of his father and elder brother. In a country where real power was no longer in the hands of the monarchy, she saw the instigators of the terrible crime going not only unpunished, but also occupying positions of influence and offices of rank. Indeed, she was brought face-to-face with them almost daily, and had to remain silent for the sake of the young King. Manuel, in the meantime, had been doing his best to rally such support as he could in parts of the country where loyalty to the throne remained strong, but he was in a tenuous position. His youth and inexperience did little to strengthen the Royalist cause, and the future of the Royal House of Braganza was in the balance.

On a personal level, he charmed and impressed everyone he met. His shy yet frank manner, fair and attractive bearing, coupled with a quick mind and fluent French and English, won him many friends. As Europe's youngest king, the gossip columnists referred to him as a 'most marriageable monarch'. In the November of 1909 he began his first round of visits to foreign courts, and was the guest of King Edward at Windsor Castle. The ease and grace with which he held his diplomatic circle was the subject of delighted comment among the ambassadors who conversed with him.

He also showed himself to be a great fan of the music halls, which must have endeared him to the British King, who had the distinction of being the first royal patron of the halls as far back as 1872.* During his week in London, Manuel managed to cram in incognito visits to the Gaiety, the Empire and to Daly's. The next stop on his tour was Paris, and naturally enough he wanted to see *Sans Rancune*, the hit revue of the season. Everybody backstage

---

* On a visit to a cattle show in 1872, King Edward, then Prince of Wales, had seen, hanging above a pen of prize pigs, a portrait of the actress Emily Soldene. He enquired who it was and was informed that she was appearing at the Philharmonic Theatre. He had never heard of this music hall, and on being told that it was situated near the Angel he remarked: 'A very good position indeed'. A week or so later he honoured the hall with a visit.

knew that he was in the theatre that night. Although Gaby did not play directly to him the whole time, she felt his eyes on her every second she was on stage. When she was presented to him after the show, the atmosphere between them was electric. Despite the King's extreme youth, and to her great surprise, she found herself attracted to him. The press may have dubbed him 'The Boy King', but the look in his eyes was direct and manly enough to make Gaby slightly embarrassed. When he told her in his impeccable French how much he had admired her performance, she could barely mumble her thanks, and hoped he had not noticed that she was blushing.

They met many times subsequently. He went again to the Capucines in the company of some wealthy Portuguese Royalists, who had fled Portugal after Kind Carlos had died. The numbers of such voluntary exiles was increasing, and there was a sizeable Portuguese colony in Paris, many of whom Gaby knew. It is therefore not inconceivable that the King and the show girl met socially in restaurants, and at the various other chic establishments where society and the *demi-mode* intermingled. By their very nature, such informal meetings between the two go unrecorded. Whether or not the young monarch took afternoon rides up to 3, rue Henri-de-Bornier is a matter for conjecture, but the affair is significant in that it was the first time that rumours linking Gaby's name with royalty had had any real substance. For the moment, these rumours were confined to Paris, where amongst Gaby's friends they became something of a joke. But the suggestion that she might be in love, albeit with someone so enormously beneficial to her career, had a softening effect on a personality that was beginning to be seen as rather hard-edged. Of course, it is easy to dismiss the whole episode as an exercise in public relations, but at this point the so-called liaison was unknown to all but a very small social circle in Paris, so it was of no direct advantage to her. Gaby continued to work in *Sans Rancune*, where her performance appeared to take on even more lustre and sparkle.

The hundredth performance of the revue was celebrated in December, when whole cast went to the Volney Restaurant, where they celebrated until 5.30 a.m. The show continued its run over Christmas and the New Year of 1910, but Gaby's time in it was drawing to a close. She was contracted to make another appearance at the Alhambra in London, and planned to go there in the spring.

In February, to her surprise and delight, she was summoned by King Manuel to appear, with various others, in Lisbon. Naturally, she was happy to oblige. There had been a huge fire in Oporto, and hundreds of families had perished and lost everything. Manuel, who counted many supporters in this nothern city, was anxious to do as much as he could to help, and planned a huge charity gala in Lisbon for the relief of the victims. Gaby said goodbye to the Capucines, packed her bags, and set out with Maman for Lisbon, where they stayed at an hotel near the gates of the palace.

For the gala, Gaby did one or two of her numbers from *Sans Rancune*, and afterwards she was presented to the formidable figure of Queen Amelie. None of the scandal linking her son to the dancer can have reached the Queen's ears, for under such circumstances she would never have consented to meet her. Gaby stayed on for a brief week in Lisbon, and then went back to Paris to make plans for her London season. The Queen went off to Biarritz in an attempt to arrange a marriage between Manuel and Princess Patricia of Connaught, a niece of King Edward VII. On her return, the scandal exploded around her. She had moved out of the Royal Palace earlier in the year, and had taken up residence at one of the other royal houses in an effort to appease critics who claimed she was exerting undue influence over the young king.

The Republican tabloids claimed that, in the Queen's absence, the King had installed Gaby Deslys in the Royal Palace. Worse still, they stated that he had presented his mistress with priceless jewels from the royal collection. Amongst these love tokens was supposed to be a row of matched pearls over eight feet in length. The Queen was horrified, even though she knew there might be little substance to the rumours, which were not the first concerning the King's love life. Only the year before, he had fallen in love with the daughter of one of the Queen's ladies-in-waiting, and had only very unwillingly discontinued the relationship at the insistence of his mother. Now, she pointed out how important it was for his country for him to make a match with a suitable royal princess from the ruling family of a powerful foreign ally.

Back in Paris, through contact with her Portuguese friends,

Gaby began to learn what Lisbon journalists were saying about her. As none of these rumours had yet reached the Paris or London press, she had no need to either confirm or deny them. Only she knew the real truth about what had happened that week in Lisbon. With this secret locked behind her pretty smile, she set off for London, and the Alhambra. Once there, once again, it seemed she could do no wrong:

> 'A major triumph.'
> 'Gaby the adorable, so pretty, so youthful.'
> '. . . her delightfully broken English never fails to bring forth laughter . . .'
> '. . . remarkable charm. The most beautiful legs in London . . .'
> '. . . her bewitching limbs . . .'

The popular press was ecstatic. *Les Caprices de Suzette* was a totally French production. Billed as a 'fantastic operetta', it was very much to the taste of the Alhambra audiences.

King Edward's taste in entertainment and a flourishing *entente cordiale* had resulted in a positive invasion of French talent. The music halls of the West End proliferated with French stars: the outrageous Polaire★ at the Palace, even the great Réjane on the variety stage at the Hippodrome.

The British monarch's death in May 1910 signalled the end of an era. Brief though his reign had been, the pleasure-loving king had done a great deal to popularise the music hall and make it, if not exactly respectable, an acceptable diversion for society. His state funeral brought to London a greater collection of crowned heads of state than would ever be seen again. The King of Portugal was among them, though his presence was hardly the subject of much attention. One cannot say whether he met Gaby or not at this time, but as she was still in London, it would have been a good opportunity. Soon afterwards, her contract with the Alhambra expired, and she departed for Paris, leaving behind her a city deep in mourning.

★ Polaire had recently returned from a tour of the United States, bringing with her an extremely young black manservant. Around his neck he wore a medallion bearing the words, 'I belong to Polaire. Please return me to her'.

For some time now, Gaby had not organized her business affairs completely alone. The financial side of her life was the one in which she took the keenest interest. She handled her own bookings as much as possible, and was not managed by any one agent. Doubtless, the hefty percentage she would have had to pay for such exclusivity would have irked her. She did have professional help in the way of accountants and lawyers, however, and was prepared to pay for the best. From the earliest times, she had displayed remarkable business acumen, and could probably have made a success of any venture.

The Alhambra contracts she had for the best part negotiated personally with Alfred Moul, and through Moul she had come into contact with his Paris booking agent, André Charlot, a man who later became one of the world's greatest producers of revue. It was due to the proximity of Charlot's office in Place Boiledieu to that of H.B. Marinelli that Gaby first seriously began to formulate plans to visit America. Marinelli was a big international agent, with offices in London, Paris and New York, as well as other major cities. Very well connected everywhere, but particularly in the United States, he handled the affairs of such diverse talents as Otéro and George Robey on their visits there, booking them with his friends the Shubert Brothers, Lee and J.J.

Marinelli had often met Gaby, and frequently tried to persuade her to go to New York, where the Shuberts were eager to present any acts that had done well in Europe. For years, Gaby declined, feeling that she wasn't quite ready. She also dreaded the thought of such a long boat trip. The rewards would have to be huge to persuade her to forget her fear of sea journeys. Even the few hours it took to cross the Channel upset her, and she always allowed herself twenty-four hours or so to recover from the ordeal. Besides which, she had so many offers to work in Paris, and had spent so little time in her own home, that now, in 1910, for a few months, she wanted to remain in one place.

Matichon was beginning to do well on the variety stage. Under the name of Kerville, she presented a singing/dancing act not unlike that of her elder sister. She was darker than Gaby, and although attractive with the same startling eyes, she could not rival her sister in looks or talent. However, she had done quite well on her own, and later, as Gaby grew more and more famous, the relationship between the two would prove a great help to Kerville's career. But for the moment she was anxious to prove her own worth, and got irritated when people referred to her as Gaby Deslys' sister. To accentuate the difference between them she darkened her hair even more, as Gaby got blonder and blonder. On a personal level, the two got on extremely well, and Gaby and Matichon were often seen out together – Matichon as beautifully dressed as Gaby, whose generosity was well-known. It was a busy summer for Gaby. She seemed to have invitations to all the best places. One of the gossip columns, reporting a party, said: 'Gaby Deslys was there. She is always everywhere, beautifully dressed and beautifully beautiful'.

Gaby was, in fact, getting to be something of a trend-setter. She was always ready to sport the latest Poiret gown, and was never happier than when given a free hand in the design of her own outfits. Whether she was patronising Doucet, Paquin or Lucile, Gaby always knew exactly what she wanted, and she had little patience with anyone who tried to dissuade her from getting it. Her style was certainly individual. Although she had not yet become as exaggerated and bizarre in the style of her dress as in later life, she was still not afraid of overstatement. Her tastes often ran to floor-length chinchilla, and flocks of stuffed rare birds on her head. Cecil Beaton went so far as to call her 'a human aviary'.

That summer of 1910, pyjamas for day wear were considered outrageously avant-garde; any form of trouser on a woman was unheard of. Most were still imprisoned in whalebone corsets that gripped them like a vice practically from knee to neck. Innovators of female fashion like Fortuny and Paul Poiret were only just beginning to free women from this restricting and ridiculous convention. For the general public, however, the sight of a woman clad in loose-fitting garments that quite obviously had no foundation other than the natural curves of the female body was shocking indeed. Thus Gaby, rehearsing her new numbers for the Folies-Bergère at Stillson's studio wearing shell-pink pyjamas made news. Stories of her liaison with Manuel had also started to filter back to London, and small items were printed in the society columns. Nothing too definite was suggested: captions such as, 'she was especially admired by the young King of Portugal on his last visit to Paris' would accompany a picture of Gaby, casual in her pyjamas, or furred, feathered and bejewelled like a latter-day Marie Antoinette.

She spent a couple of months rehearsing for the new Folies-Bergère revue, where she would be top of the bill, but in the end she did not take part at all, due to a combination of contractual difficulties and further problems with her throat. The chest colds she was prone to always affected her throat. Her voice suffered greatly from these onslaughts, so she tried hard to make singing the least important part of her act. She had even learnt mime from George Wagne, who had also taught Colette, and had presented this with great success on her last visit to the Alhambra. Whatever the reasons were for her not going ahead with the Folies revue, Otéro took her place in it, and Gaby went off to Vienna, arriving there in September. It was a sensational season in more ways than one.

Vienna at this time was one of the entertainment capitals of the world. A city associated with popular music since the heady days of the waltz, it was a wild, gay place, buzzing with nightlife, its cafés, bars and theatres rivalling any in Paris for colour and vivacity. The Apollo Theatre was the Viennese equivalent of London's Alhambra, a large, fashionable hall where the cream of society gathered nightly to watch a show packed with the biggest names in European and American variety, acts who were happy to make the long trek east for the financial rewards. Gaby's dressing room was often besieged with admirers, their visiting cards and baskets of flowers making it look like an expensive florists. As more arrived, Gaby would give them away to her dressers, girls in the chorus, the local hospital; everyone benefitted from her generosity.

On the first night at the Apollo, accompanied by various members of her retinue, Gaby left the stage door, and was greeted by the usual throng of autograph-hunters and well-wishers. Suddenly, a small peasant woman dressed in black detached herself from the crowd, approached Gaby, and, pulling the sleeve of her chinchilla coat, cried out, 'Hedy, Hedy!' with tears coursing down her lined face. Gaby pulled back, startled, and the woman started talking rapidly and emotionally in a dialect that she later discovered to be Bohemian. The unknown woman became a frequent visitor to the stage door, and began to make a nuisance of herself. She begged to be allowed to see Gaby privately, insisting that the actress was her daughter, and weeping copious tears when refused access to the star dressing room. Her name was Madame Navratil, and though she stopped coming to the theatre after a week or so, Gaby had not heard the last of her.

In the first week of October, this minor occurrence and all others were eclipsed by the bombshell that burst on Gaby's life. There was a bloody and violent revolution in Portugal. Reports from Lisbon talked of a city in chaos, of fires everywhere, 'not a window left unbroken'. Pictures of the King were being burned in the streets. The Royal Palace itself had been attacked and looted; priceless works of art and antiquities were destroyed or stolen. The King and other members of the Royal Family had escaped with their lives – but only just.

A dinner party was in progress when the revolution broke out. The King and his mother were hastily smuggled out of the Palace by Loyalists as the Republicans were approaching. They were hustled aboard the royal yacht *Amelia* without having had time to pack even the smallest bag. The loyal captain had rapidly recruited a crew consisting mostly of fishermen, and the yacht sped off into the night as fires began to light up the sky above Lisbon. A cheering, victorious mob stormed the Palace to find it empty, the King and his party gone. Food was still on dinner plates, candles sputtered in ornate candelabra, as the first bombs shattered the windows.

Pandemonium reigned. Dawn broke on a city battered, bloody and smoking. Bodies of both Loyalists and insurgents littered the streets; the Republican flag, defiant and victorious, fluttered from government buildings, some of which were reduced to charred ruins. Dawn also saw the disembarkation of a strangely garbed, pale and shaken royal party at Gibraltar. Most of them were still in evening dress, with the crew's sweaters thrown over the top. It was a sad day for the young King, another tragedy in a life that had already seen so much. In Vienna, Gaby burst into tears on hearing the news. She was particularly upset to discover her young royal friend had sustained slight injury, but at least he had escaped alive. The revolution made headline news all over the world. In England it even ousted the Crippen murder case from the front pages.

42

From this day on, the life of Gaby Deslys changed drastically. The small and discreet references to her relationship with the King, that had peppered the gossip columns of the cheaper newspapers in Europe, became banner headlines. Some continental publications went as far as blaming her directly for the revolution. Great indignation, these journalists stated, had been caused of late in Lisbon by the way in which the King had maintained his friendship with Gaby Deslys without taking the least precaution to conceal his infatuation. His conduct in giving her jewels of enormous value when Portugal was almost bankrupt, and was groaning under many abuses, excited the keenest resentment. She was the straw that broke the camel's back. Although the more conservative press in Britain chose to ignore this scandal, the foreign press was not so restrained.* In America, Gaby Deslys became a household name overnight. Bold black headlines declared her to be the 'Siren that cost a King his throne'. Every detail of the affair was printed and exaggerated out of all proportion. Gaby, who had maintained total silence over the friendship, was besieged in her hotel in Vienna by pressmen from all over the world. She was finally forced to make a public statement. After giving brief details of their meeting in Paris and her subsequent trip to Lisbon, she answered her critics who maintained that the King had got into financial difficulties over her:

'These suspicions are entirely unfounded. He is such a good boy, intelligent and most religious. To tax Manuel with luxuriousness and setting a bad example is the worst hypocrisy. His presents to me were no more than the average bourgeois would give. The truth is that my own income is considerably larger than his. I am just starting for Berlin where Bendiner, the variety lessee, is paying me £4,650 for a three-month engagement. I have kept my friendship with the King a secret, and have consistently denied it until recent developments made it impossible. Just fancy, a big manager has had the impudence since the revolution broke out to wire me an offer of £4,000 to appear on the Lisbon stage for just six weeks!

* The British press has always been reluctant to divulge the private affairs of royalty, and not just its own. Years later, the British public were the last to learn of the affair between the Prince of Wales and Mrs Wallis Simpson.

'My reason for indignantly spurning a contract in a Parisian revue was that I was required to appear as the King's fiancée. Another actress was engaged who assumed my name and presented herself on stage leaning on the Boy King's arm. I protested to the managers, who then spread the report that I had quit the stage and had contracted a morganatic marriage with the King of Portugal. I took my pen and dispatched to the newspapers this declaration – "Gabrielle Deslys has no desire to descend from the throne she actually occupies today. She is a queen in the great world of Art, whereas Portugal is but a petty state".'

It is hard to imagine that she was being serious, and the pompous folly of this statement, hitherto unreported in England, did not go unnoticed by British society journals. The *Tatler* said:

'Mlle Deslys calls herself "a Queen of the World of Art", but in her case it is certainly a teeny-weeny little world. She is quite pretty of course, and she dances neatly, and the little upward curl of her mouth, so assiduously cultivated, is very fetching for a short time; but to turn her nose up at a real kingdom merely because one has a certain celebrity in the music-hall world is surely the very height of ridiculous feminine vanity to which an equally ridiculous public can encourage one of its pretty favourites.'

In a later issue they detailed the affair, and said: 'The lady, whose dark, provocative eyes shine out in a pseudo–childlike fashion from under a straight cut golden fringe . . . found the merest child's play the allurement of a sentimental boy.' Whatever the sanctimonious criticisms of an ungrateful press, who had from Gaby's career gained untold column inches of news, the immediate effect on her life was cataclysmic. The Apollo Theatre in Vienna was jammed full to the roof every night, and the hubbub surrounding her reached fever pitch in the weeks following the revolution. Even the simple mechanics of going to and from the theatre required careful subterfuge, her driver making sure he left at different times and took different routes to avoid the world's press who clamoured for interviews every hour of the day.

In the midst of all this chaos, Gaby managed to make some

recordings* – her first and last. It was a publicist's dream. The thrill Gaby had felt when she had seen her first full-page picture in the *Sketch* should have been magnified a thousand times when she saw her photograph in an American journal, accompanied by the caption, 'Gaby, the most talked-about woman in the world'. She only wished she felt well enough to enjoy it.

Gaby had ample time to take stock of her life during the winter of 1910. Her doctors had ordered her to rest, for she was physically and mentally exhausted. Glad to leave the hubbub of Vienna behind her, she set off for Monte Carlo, where, in her native Mediterranean sun, she could spend a few weeks refuelling her energies and planning her future. Although still young, her thirtieth birthday found her pondering how much longer she could go on at this pace. Never had so many opportunities been open to her; never had she felt so incapable of taking advantage of any of them. As she lay on her bed, looking through the hotel window at the blue southern skies, she was haunted again by the spectre of the aged actress, alone, sick, poor and unloved. Gaby fell into a deep, uncharacteristic depression. She had achieved fame beyond her wildest dreams, but at the expense of her privacy. Some days she wished she had done as her father wanted; married a nice bourgeois boy, settled down in Marseilles and had a family.

She regretted having never had a deep emotional involvement. Her hectic professional life had allowed her time only for fleeting affairs. She had never met anyone she really cared about, with the exception of poor Manuel, and even then she did not trust her own emotions, could never really say that her feelings were untainted by self-interest. She determined that, if her public image prevented her from leading a normal private life, then she would make as much money from it as she could. If her voice went (and some days the pain in her throat was so bad she could hardly speak), she would give the audiences something else that would keep them

* These three recordings, *Tout en Rose, Philomène* and *La Parisienne* were made for the London branch of HMV by Franz Hampe on 15 October 1910. *Tout en Rose* and *La Parisienne* were issued on one record, *Philomène* by itself, and though copies of these still exist, they are extremely rare. Gaby's voice is revealed to be surprisingly operatic; her perfect pitch showing that her years at the conservatoire were not wasted.

clamouring to see her. But most important of all, she decided she was not going to kill herself for the sake of some fat, cigar-smoking impresario.

If they wanted her – and at that moment the theatrical managers of the world were desperate to cash in on her 'notoriety' – they would have to pay. She in turn would give them a performance worth every penny, dazzling her audiences with a unique display of glamour, riches, style and daring. But first, she knew she must get her obligations in Europe out of the way, so that she could conquer America, and strike while the scandal was still hot.

The rest had done her good. Fuelled by her resolve, she made her way back to Paris to put her plans into practice.

6

ALTERED VALUES

Back in Paris, managers were scrambling to get Gaby to appear in their theatres. She was considering the many offers being made to her when, suddenly, in late December 1910, she made a totally unexplained visit to London. It may be that she went to discuss an offer from a London theatre, but as she was still under contract to the Alhambra it seems unlikely. And as ex-King Manuel was in London at this time, there is a distinct possibility that she went to visit him. While in London, she read an article that *Comoedia Illustré* had printed in Paris, to the effect that she was so unhappy about the accusations of her role in the King's downfall, that she had attempted suicide. She sent them a cable which they printed: *Je n'ai nulle envie de me suicider. Dîtes-le croyez-le et croyez moi. Bien votre, Gaby Deslys.*★

Alfred Moul was eager to get her back to the Alhambra for the following winter season, under the terms of her old contract, and when she returned to Paris after her mysterious trip to London, André Charlot set about trying to arrange this. He had several meetings with Gaby, one of which he found particularly upsetting. He reported the details back to Moul:

> April 7th 1911
> *André Charlot to Alfred Moul*
>
> Dear Mr Moul,
>
> I wish I could stereograph my interview with Gaby Deslys because I would not like to forget any part of it.
>
> I have seen and communicated to her what you said in your letter of the 5th inst.
>
> She then told me: 'I have not yet answered Mr Moul because I have been busy with my rehearsals. It is impossible for me to

★'I have no wish to kill myself, say it, believe it, believe me. Best wishes, Gaby Deslys.'

open two weeks earlier, in fact I don't know if I will open in London at all.

'The contract I have with Mr Moul is a very old one, and the salary is simply ridiculous. In Paris I can earn twenty pounds per day and all my costumes are paid for by the management. In London I have to pay a singer, a dancer, the costumes and a royalty to the author of the sketch and my hotel expenses.

'What shall it leave me at the end of each week compared with what I can get in America?

'I am offered in New York one thousand dollars per day for myself alone; why should I go to London for one hundred and twenty-five pounds per week with all the expenses I have there?

'It would be more profit for me to pay Mr Moul the six weeks' salary I owe him if I break the contract and go to New York; I would earn in less than a week what I owe the Alhambra.'

I then told her that if she did such a thing as break her contract you had clauses in it barring her from playing in London.

She answered that she did not care, and that she had more offers throughout the world than she could ever play.

I then asked her what she wanted. She told me: 'If Mr Moul is not willing to raise my salary, I shall either pay him the amount of six weeks for breaking the contract or I shall go on and do a six-minute turn singing one song and the Alhambra will never see me again.

'If Mr Moul is willing to raise my salary by forty pounds per week and pay the singer himself I will play the eight weeks and consider his offers for the future.

'But you must tell Mr Moul my value has altered a lot since I signed the contract, and if I ask him only forty pounds per week more it is because he is very nice, and I want him to be pleased, but in fact I should ask him for much, much more, as I could get eighteen hundred francs per day from the Palace.'

PS: I have read this through again, it is exactly what she said, but the way I have written it you would think she had talked to me roughly – on the contrary, she addressed me very nicely, and although the things she said were not at all nice to hear, she said them in a most charming way.

I do not think she would pay for the cancelled contract as she does not like to get rid of money. She made the same offer to the Folies-Bergère, but when they agreed to take the money she never sent it.

A.C.

The rehearsals that Gaby mentioned were for a new revue at the small but fashionable Capucines Theatre. After her success there in *Sans Rancune*, she had established a good rapport with the director, Armand Berthez, and it was his offer that she had accepted from the many possibilities open to her. Paris in the spring of 1911 was buzzing with talk about Gaby Deslys, and her reappearance on the tiny stage of the Capucines was eagerly awaited.

In between rehearsals for this, she was interviewed and photographed apparently without end. The photographs show her wearing the most sumptuous dresses imaginable: tightly fitting sheaths, beaded and sequinned in complex designs, slashed to the knees; shapely legs clothed in embroidered silk stockings; the little feet in brocaded shoes with the highest possible heels; her full bust spilling over the top of a plunging neckline; a fortune in osprey feathers atop her head; and massive pearls everywhere, at her throat, on her fingers, rows of them even looped around her beaded cap. She gazes imperiously over her shoulder – aloof, beautiful, unapproachable and alone.

It was rumoured that her relationship with Manuel continued. Alleged sightings of the couple occurred at the theatre, in the Bois de Boulogne, even at costumiers preparing her outfits for the new London revue, negotiations for which André Charlot had managed finally to complete after months of wrangling. He and Alfred Moul had been desperate to get her, and she knew it. Charlot had become increasingly exasperated with her. One of the letters he wrote to Moul says: 'She is assisted by a very clever lawyer . . . of course her terms are prohibitive, she thinks of nothing but money now'. But even if the Alhambra could not hope to match the offers she was getting from other theatres, Gaby could negotiate all sorts of other perks, and she did. In return for all their concessions, she promised Charlot and Moul a sketch that would make everyone sit up, something that no one had ever done before.

While she had been lying ill in Monte Carlo a few months earlier,

49

she told the doctor that she had so much work to do, she really could not afford the time to lie in bed. He replied that, if she didn't take care of herself a bit better, she would have to do her show in bed. She had laughed weakly, but the doctor's little joke had stuck in her mind, and she thought, 'Why not?'

She planned then that the action of her next sketch in London should take place in her boudoir, which was outrageous for the times. Of course, Gaby's was to be no ordinary boudoir. After Charlot and Alfred Moul had (grudgingly) agreed to pay, she commissioned Charles Bernel to arrange the stage properties. Bernel was an antique dealer with one of the smartest galleries in Paris with whom she had become great friends. He had guided her taste, and with his help, her house at rue Henri-de-Bornier had become a showplace of elegance and chic. Now, together they planned the smartest stage boudoir possible, featuring original eighteenth-century furnishings, hangings, chandeliers and pictures. The bed itself, a vast, gilded four-poster, was to be a line-for-line copy of one at the Palace of Versailles made for Marie Antoinette. Charlot groaned when he heard the cost; the bed alone would cost over £1,000. But Alfred Moul knew the investment would pay off, and he was right.

This first ever 'bedroom sketch' caused a sensation; business was so good that, after the first week or so, extra seats were installed in the auditorium in every available space. Gaby was happy to be back in London. The audiences were far less restrained here than in Paris, especially as her last appearances there had been at the Capucines, whose small, fashionable audience did not even like to applaud. At the Alhambra, Gaby felt a rapport with her audience that spurred her to new heights. She was funny, sexy and coquettish, and romped her way with relish through her new piece, which was called *Les Débuts de Chichine*.

The plot was rather flimsy, and involved interaction between Chichine, a professional beauty who aspired to the stage, and her three lovers. She cannot make up her mind which one she wants: a singer who lives in the apartment above her, a dancer who lives in the one below, or an Englishman who is just a visitor with lots of money and contacts. Of course, in the end she chooses the Englishman, who has managed to get one of his friends to offer her

The rising starlet – Gaby in Paris, 1902

Gaby at the Paris Scala, 1904

In *Les Caprices du Suzette* in Vienna at the time of the Manuel scandal

The starfish costume from *Aladdin*, Gaiety Theatre, 1906

The Gaiety Theatre

From *À La Carte*. Cecil Beaton described Gaby as 'A Human Aviary'

'The Charm of Paris' from *Aladdin*, Gaiety Theatre, 1906

The Ju Jitsu Waltz from *Aladdin*. Gaby with
Yukio Tani. Gaiety Theatre, 1906

Marigny Theatre, Paris 1912

Publicity shot, 1912. Even some Parisians were
shocked

Harry Pilcer and Gaby, publicity shot 1913

Endorsing Odol mouthwash, 1907

Gaby, *circa* 1912

Gaby and Barrie caricatured in *5064 Gerrard*. Robert Hale is on the right

Publicity shot designed to enhance Gaby's racy reputation, Paris 1912

Ex-king Manuel's wedding

Gordon Selfridge, *circa* 1917

a contract. In the meantime, there is all sorts of farcical business between Gaby and the other two. Her character never does get to bed, being constantly interrupted by one or the other of her suitors, and even at one point having her attempts at slumber ruined by finding a (real) cat and two tiny kittens hidden in between the sheets. Not, however, that she could possibly have hoped to get any sleep in the elaborate nightdresses in which she played the scenes – festooned with jewels and bits of hanging tulle. Offstage and on, she became an enormous celebrity; her suite at the Savoy was the meeting place for the theatrical 'glitterati' of the era. She may have had a reputation as being a hard bargainer with managements, but her lavish generosity towards everyone else surrounding her became legendary.

In the meantime, Manuel and Queen Amelie had set up home in England at Wood Norton, near Evesham, Worcestershire, the seat of her brother, the Duke of Orléans. Although glad to have escaped from Portugal alive, the young King found life in his uncle's home somewhat stifling. The vast house, greatly enlarged by the Duke, boasted fortifications that would have been better suited to an island stronghold than to the house of an English gentleman situated in the heart of the Worcestershire countryside. A wall of galvanised iron, ten feet high and topped with spikes, surrounded the property which the Duke had inherited from his uncle, the Duke D'Aumale, son of King Louis Philippe. When the monarchy finally crumbled in France, the King's eldest son migrated to England, and built a modest house on a rather barren tract of land surrounded by hills. He had a passion for landscaping, and by the time he died and the property was inherited by his great-nephew, a great forest had grown up around the house. As a keen rider and brilliant shot, he had also made himself an extremely popular local figure.

On his death, the property passed to the Duke of Orléans, and the whole situation changed. The Duke, who possessed a far keener sense of his family's importance than did his predecessor, began to detach himself from local society. He added considerably to the house, and now, by the time Manuel and his mother arrived, long corridors and galleries linked one high-ceilinged chamber to another, and the dark-panelled walls were hung with hundreds of trophy heads and specimens testifying to their owner's skill with a

GD-3

rifle. It was a gloomy mausoleum, and although the Queen was probably happy to be back in what was, after all, her family home, the oppressive atmosphere and omnipresence of his uncle soon made Manuel eager to establish himself somewhere in his own right.

The search for a suitable bride continued. To escape the tedium of life at Wood Norton, he would often disappear to London. He became quite a familiar sight in the West End, where the music halls, theatres and fashionable restaurants welcomed him, for his tragic accession and rapid deposition had captured public imagination and sympathy. Fond as ever of musical comedy, he twice went to Daly's to see Lily Elsie play the title role in *The Dollar Princess*. The pretty young actress who had not been considered a big enough draw to carry off Gertie Millar's part in *The New Aladdin* had spent the last five years making a name for herself, and was at the peak of her success. Later, like so many of her kind, she made a good society marriage, becoming Mrs Ian Bullough in 1912.

According to Jaques-Charles, Manuel also took advantage of these excursions to renew his acquaintance with Gaby. She had suffered a relapse of her illness through strenuous overwork, and had moved out of the Savoy to a small flat nearby. Jacques-Charles was in London at the time and helped nurse her. She was very grateful, and told him: 'If ever you need anything, you only need to ask'. It was to be years before he would take up her offer. It was at this flat that the young ex-King came to visit her. Their meetings were held in deepest secrecy: when Manuel was expected, the house would be emptied completely, with only Madame Caire remaining to receive him and take him to her daughter. In public, Gaby refused to talk about him. She was always happy to be interviewed and photographed, but this one subject was taboo.

In the spring of 1911, she finally succumbed to offers made via H. B. Marinelli to do a season in America for the Shubert Brothers. Lee and J. J. (Jake) Shubert were among the handful of American showmen following the lead of the great Florenz Ziegfeld in producing the first spectacular revues in American form. These revues, forerunners of the American stage musicals that became an art form later in the century, were almost a marriage between burlesque and vaudeville, but much refined, and decorated with imported star turns. But whereas Ziegfeld was an artist producing shows of great taste and beauty, the Shuberts were entrepreneurs who were only interested in making big money by pandering to the American public. After recent events, one of the things the American public wanted was Gaby Deslys.

The Americans, often more interested in royalty than Europeans, were fascinated by the King Manuel affair. The story of the sudden and dramatic infatuation of a ruling monarch for a French *danseuse* provided a major sensation for the American press and their millions of readers. Every movement made by Gaby Deslys and the King was chronicled, and, when the real facts were not available, complete fiction was published instead.

Gaby never had to seek publicity in America, she was already famous. Long articles had appeared for months, giving every detail of what she looked like, what she wore, her face, her figure and, most of all, her jewellery, listed down to the last seed pearl and diamond chip. She was called 'The uncrowned queen of the European stage', 'The most famous professional beauty in the world' and, rather delightfully, 'Gaby-of-the-fortune-round-the-neck'. She was made the heroine of a romantic royal love story, or alternatively the blood-sucking adventuress, out to rob a foolish young king of his royal jewels. Sadly, she was frequently described as 'The dancer who brought about the fall of a monarchy', and this story was believed by millions.

The Shuberts had been trying to sign her purely on her theatrical merits as far back as 1908, but now they were desperately keen. Jake Shubert came over personally to try and persuade her. When, in Marinelli's Paris office, he finally secured her signature on a contract, it was a stiff one. Gaby demanded, and got, a salary of $4,000 a week, plus travelling expenses for her whole party, plus an allowance for costumes, plus $10,000 in advance. There was even an escape clause stating that, should she, for urgent personal reasons, have to return to Europe, then the contract would be void. The contract, for three tours over a three-year period, with her weekly wage rising by $1,000 each year, was cast-iron, and weighted completely on her side. Shubert later justified giving her all this by saying, 'I'm paying her four thousand dollars a week when I can gross twenty thousand. That means with six thousand dollars running expenses, I can clear ten thousand dollars. She's cheap at the price.' He went back to New York to prepare the ground. When he announced that Gaby would be coming over for that winter season, there was an immediate rush from ticket agencies that reimbursed him for his advance several times over.

The US deal proved big enough to make Gaby overcome her fear of sea crossings. The plan the Shuberts had was to lift the whole production of *Chichine*, lock, stock and gilded bedstead to New York for a short season, and then, towards Christmas, to put Gaby into an entirely new production they were devising, an operetta called *Vera Violetta*.

Gaby could not wait. Many preparations had to be made, vast new wardrobes of clothes had to be acquired. Maison Lewis had prepared a collection of astonishing hats for her. The current fashion in headgear dictated that, after years of getting wider and wider, hats would now slim down and become taller and taller instead. Gaby made sure that she had dozens of these 'skyscraper' hats, considering them particularly appropriate for her first American season.

She was interviewed by the British press, with whom her accessibility made her a great favourite. Though not as accessible to anyone else she would always see a reporter. She was probably the first international star to realize the importance of publicity, and to take full advantage of it. One or two others had thought up the occasional stunt (including Anna Held, who had milk churns delivered to her suite in the Savoy to further the legend that daily milk baths were responsible for the beauty of her complexion) but in America Gaby Deslys' fame was completely founded on pre-publicity. She hoped that she could live up to the legend she had created for herself.

7

THE TIGER AND
THE BUTTERFLY

One Saturday night in September the same year, 1911, she was sitting in a box at the Winter Garden theatre waiting for the curtain to go up, still wondering if she could live up to the expectations she had aroused in the U.S. She had only arrived that morning, but had got straight down to work by going to take a look at the theatre in which she would be performing.

She certainly felt like a somebody. The dress she had chosen for her first night out in America made sure of that. The gold in her hair, and the green of her eyes, were picked out in the figured silk brocade of her gown. Black silk gauze only partially covered generous expanses of her bosom and back. One of Lewis's Juliet caps sat on her blonde head, black and beaded, trimmed with matching *aigrettes* of the finest quality, flaring dangerously towards the red-shaded wall lights. She toyed rather nervously with the fat rows of glistening pearls cascading down to her lap, the even larger solitaires on her fingers catching the light as she did so.

She looked down on the audience. Dozens of pairs of opera glasses were turned towards her. People were waving and smiling as if they knew her. The Americans certainly were not shy. She could hear her name being whispered, its sibilant syllables discernible above the sound of the orchestra tuning up.

It had been a long day, and the culmination of a long trip. That morning, when her ship, the *Lorraine* finally slipped into the dock at New York, after hours of delay due to unseasonably heavy fog, Gaby had been surprised at her reception. The Shuberts had done their work well, everyone knew she was coming. A message had even been sent to shore from the ship's wireless to announce her arrival. Cheers of 'Gaby!' were heard as she appeared on deck. She stepped daintily down the gangplank, a retinue of maids, assistants and porters struggling behind her with the twenty-seven steamer trunks bearing her initials. The first person she saw was her old friend Fred Wright from the Moulin Rouge. It was good to see one friendly, familiar face amongst so many strange ones.

Jake Shubert was also there, as well as various other management people: lawyers, publicists, dozens of photographers, the full circus. She had never known anything like it, and was both elated and terrified until the actress in her took over. Then, at the photographers' request, she lifted the white veil covering her face, smiled her brilliant smile, and patiently posed while cameras clicked and everyone talked at once, dozens of pencils scribbling down her every utterance, every detail of her blue satin coat with its lace trim, and her embroidered stockings. 'Show us your pearls, Gaby!' 'One more big smile over here, please!' they cried. She allowed herself to be directed, laughingly opening her coat to reveal the ropes of pearls that formed so important a part of her myth. She was guided over to the customs house, where another ordeal awaited her. The customs appraiser needed details of everything she had brought; needed to know which costumes were for stage wear, which were her own, and how much everything was worth. Three of the trunks were kept back for further examination, and with the remaining twenty-four she made her way to the St Regis Hotel, and her first American press conference.

Everything she saw on the ride to the hotel amazed her. The long, straight streets lined with incredibly tall buildings, the elevated railway, and more automobiles than she had ever dreamt existed. In the St Regis, the pressmen were full of questions, although at the very first mention of King Manuel, her newly acquired press agent announced that Miss Deslys had nothing whatever to say about him, but that they could ask her anything else. She told them about the sketch she was to appear in, how her English audiences had loved it, and that she hoped her American ones would do the same. She was startled at the frankness of the questions they asked: 'How much are your pearls worth, Gaby?', 'Are you a natural blonde?' Nevertheless, it was easy, with her halting English, to pretend that she had not understood any questions she did not like. It would take a little practice, but she knew she would soon learn to handle American newsmen as surely as she could an audience.

It did not take her long to find out that the dollar ruled here, in the Land of the Free; that the word 'free' implied the right to go make as much money as you possibly could. And the fact that she had made so much was one of the reasons why people were fascinated by her. There was a constant emphasis on money. The theatrical trade paper, *Variety*, published weekly the exact nightly takings in the major theatres, as well as details of performers' salaries. Nothing was sacrosanct. It was common knowledge that Gaby was earning $4,000 a week, a fact that excited the keenest resentment in some quarters. *Variety* stated baldly that it did not think she was worth it. For that money, it said, she might at least have a picture of King Manuel hanging in the boudoir stage set of *Chichine*, with which she opened at the Winter Garden on 27 September 1911. And it did not even like the sketch, considering it too racy.

'It may be considered *au fait* for Frenchmen to make love in the bedchamber of their adored while she is attired in a short night robe, but America doesn't believe in the system,' said the magazine. Its writers also thought, 'Gaby has brought over a capable company, as she should have at the price'. Gaby read this angrily. 'Anyone would think they were paying my wages,' she is reported to have said. The Shuberts, who *were* paying her wages, utilised her the way they normally did their expensive star acts. A whole host of cheap, second-rate turns were used to pad out the bill, so that, to quote *Variety*, 'The audience had to sit through a load of junk' before seeing their star. This sometimes had disastrous consequences, as Gaby was to find out.

Although there was much talent in the new Shubert show, *Vera Violetta*, it had some serious flaws. The Shuberts always conducted practice runs in the provinces for their major productions, and *Vera Violetta* was first staged at the Hyperion, New Haven, on 19 November 1911. It proved to be the most humiliating night of Gaby's career. The audience consisted largely of students from Yale College, who were already in an ugly mood before the curtain went up. They had suffered an ignominious defeat that afternoon on the football field at the hands of their arch rivals, Princeton. Further bad feeling was caused by the fact that tickets for the show had risen to $3. The interminable length of the show – over two and half hours – proved too much, especially as the star turns had been kept for immediately after the interval.

When the curtain went up on the second act, the audience was unprepared to give anyone a chance, and jeers and catcalls greeted Gaby's entrance. She was stunned. It had been obvious from the atmosphere in the first half that there might be trouble ahead, but nothing had prepared her for this. She thought of her first night at the Gaiety so many years ago, when she had thought the boos and jeers were directed at her. Tonight they were meant for everybody. She stood frozen to the spot. A few moments passed, but the booing and hissing and cries of 'Get off!' grew louder. The first missile, an apple core, struck her on the leg, galvanizing her into action. She ran into the wings, tears coursing down her face, as the sound of seats being ripped up rent the air. It was a full-scale riot. Backstage everything was in turmoil. The manager called the police, and warned everyone to stay in their dressing rooms, and to lock the doors.

Gaby was terrified. What kind of country was this where they wrecked the theatre if they did not like the show? Slowly, as the police arrived, and the sounds of the battle in the auditorium filled her ears, her fear turned to anger. No amount of money could recompense her for this humiliation. She was going home. Back in London and Paris her audience adored her, they would never believe this had happened. The next day, on the train back to New York, she was still in a rage. The other members of the cast seemed to take it all in their stride, said the 'Yalies' had all had too much to drink and were furious at losing their match in the afternoon. The show needed trimming down anyway, they said. Wait 'til Monday. The Winter Garden will be a different ball game. Gaby, still shaken, swore she was going to leave and never come back to America. Back at the St Regis, she had time to calm down and reflect. Why should she give in? The Winter Garden was, after all, a different ball game . . .

When the show did open there the following Monday, Gaby found that her biggest problem was not with the audience, but with one of her fellow performers. In such a competitive business, with everyone struggling to get to the top of the bill, she had to deal with some very large egos. The largest of all belonged to a young man determined to succeed at all costs. His name was Al Jolson, and *Vera Violetta* was one of his first Broadway shows. Jolson was determined that nothing was going to stand in his way, least of all this small Frenchwoman, who could not even sing, and who hardly spoke the language. Rehearsals were difficult, to say the least. Patient though the other members of the cast were with her, Jolson lost no opportunity to show the dislike and resentment he felt towards her and her huge salary. Even during public performances, he would upstage her ruthlessly, clowning and making faces behind her back when they were on stage together, taking every opportunity to distract the audience and belittle her performance.

Tough though she had become, Gaby was no match for him. She shed many tears of frustrated rage, and there were times when she felt like leaving the production. It is indicative of her strength of character that she did not give in, consoling herself with the knowledge that she was, after all, the star of the show. Despite her dislike of him, she watched Jolson's performance, and noted with awe his remarkable ability to seduce the audience. Even though his big, powerful voice had no difficulty in reaching the furthest seats in the auditorium, even before microphones were invented, he would make sure that everyone got to hear him by leaping off the stage and running up and down the aisles, singing and clowning all the way. To compare him with Gaby would be like comparing a butterfly with a tiger. In a competition to see who could make the most noise, she stood no chance. But it was not her voice that interested people – they had come to see the legend, the beautiful butterfly that had captured a king. So Gaby let the tiger roar, and concentrated her energies on giving the crowd something Jolson never could, and every night her gorgeous costumes, jewels and radiant blonde beauty won her a standing ovation.

In fact, Jolson was one of the few people who did not love her and appreciate her act. She had many friends in the company willing to give her affection and encouragement to counterbalance his open aggression. One of these friends, José Collins, recalled in her memoirs how lonely she was feeling, having also just arrived in this foreign country from London, when, on the first day of rehearsals, she was sitting in the wings:

> 'For the sake of picturesqueness in my story I should have, at this stage, burst into a flood of tears. Probably I would have done so had not a dazzling little figure with large, magnetic eyes come tripping across the stage to the corner where I was struggling with my lines. I recognised her at once from photographs I had seen of her – it was little Gaby Deslys. With her quick, sudden smiles and little ingratiating ways and witty chatter, she immediately made me feel at home, and in five minutes we were devoted friends. She fascinated me intensely – she was so scintillating, so vital in her movements and gestures, so immensely understanding and sympathetic – so somehow pathetic too.'

Gaby also had a tremendous admiration for José, a singer who had inherited the talent of her mother, Lottie Collins, a music-hall star of the previous generation. José continues:

> 'Gaby used to stand in the wings night after night to hear me sing, and would shout "Bravo, José!" when I finished each number. Then, as I came off, she would rush up to me and exclaim, "Oh, what I wouldn't give to be able to sing like that!" Gaby simply adored and lived for her work. She was in her practice clothes from morning until night trying to improve her dancing. She wanted to be able to give something better in her dancing every day, like the great little artiste she was. Her generosity, of course, was proverbial. She would give away anything she possessed. There wasn't a spark of jealousy in her, just admiration for anyone who had any talent.'

This generosity was at direct odds with a newspaper statement Gaby gave at this time, concerning her attitude to money. A remarkable document, it is hard to imagine any actress, past or present, displaying such candour, and is worth quoting extensively. The *New York Journal* had published an article written by Alan Dale, denouncing Gaby as a heartless adventuress. This is her very frank reply:

> 'I am called mercenary – your Alan Dale has said that all I love is the dollar; and all I think of is money! They say, too, that I cannot love; that I am too hard, too fond of money to love!

60

'I *am* mercenary! I *do* love money! I take all I can and keep all I get! I give nothing back.

'I can love. It is in me to have that grand passion, but first I must make my fortune. When I have all the money I want, then I will marry, and when I marry it will be for all time. Gaby Deslys will never figure in a divorce!

'The world will take all a woman has and will give her nothing in return if she asks for nothing. But let her fix her price and stand by it, and the world will give her all she wants, and ask to give her more.

'When youth passes, when beauty goes, money is the only thing that helps a woman against the world. The rich woman has a natural barrier between herself and the world! Men pay more respect to my pearls than to my beauty or my talent!

'An artiste's vogue soon passes. Other favourites cast her to one side. She has saved no money. She has not got the worth for what she has been. She has, perhaps, been dazzled with "generosity". No woman can afford to be generous with the world. The world laughs and takes and says – what you call it here – "Easy thing!" A woman who is generous with the world is a fool, and the world knows she is a fool and strips her.

'Men say I am beautiful, I am magnetic. It may be true. If it is, then let me make the most of it. These are things of worth. If I give men the pleasures of them, men must pay for them. Beauty goes, magnetism fails. Money alone remains, if you are careful.

'Men expect me to give them my time for nothing. They expect me to sup with them, dine with them. My time is money. Any man who has a hundred, two hundred dollars in his pocket thinks he can invite me to supper! Peef! I laugh. If I want supper I can buy it for myself. I refuse. They sneer and say – "The little miser! The mercenary!"

'There are few men whose company could compensate me for my loss of time!

'When I arrived in New York a man who lives on Fifth Avenue sent me a very big basket of American Beauty roses; it reached from the floor to the ceiling. It must have cost a hundred, two hundred dollars. I did not know him. *He did not know me*! I saw supper, dinner, written on every leaf. Foolish man!

'Did I send them back? No, but no! I keep all I get, I give nothing back!'

61

She was ahead of her time. These frankly feminist sentiments can have done little to endear her to American manhood, and eventually did her a great deal of harm. But she was at least totally honest, and in presenting herself as one woman against the world, presaged a whole school of feminist thought that was as yet not even fully conceived. With reference to her declarations about being capable of love, the veracity of these statements was about to be realized sooner than she thought.

One of the featured dancers in *Vera Violetta* was a young man called Harry Pilcer. Gaby was immediately attracted to him. He was short, dark and handsome, and about the same age and height as her. He was the eldest son of an Austro-Hungarian Jewish tailor, who had emigrated to the United States while he was still very young. The family grew in America, and now Harry had six brothers and sisters. His father had wanted him to enter the family business, but he had other ideas.

By the age of seven, Harry knew he wanted to be a performer; by his teens he was working as a chorus boy on Broadway. In 1911 he was an accomplished, and often featured, dancer. Called upon to partner Gaby, it became immediately apparent that, at least as dance partners, they were made for each other. Long years of practice had made Gaby a reasonable dancer, but Harry was a brilliantly innovative artist whose uniquely American style took her, and later Europe, by storm. They were so good together that the Shuberts let Pilcer write and choreograph some new numbers for them, one of which Pilcer called 'The Gaby Glide.' Rather ungraceful though this number was – a kind of jazzed-up but less violent 'Apache'* dance – the rhythm was exciting, and the way the couple moved together enthused audiences greatly, and got everyone talking.

They went everywhere together: Harry no doubt tickled pink at being seen around with such a famous figure; Gaby quite open

---

* The 'Apache', or *Valse chaloupée*, was introduced at the Moulin Rouge in 1908 by Max Déarly and Mistinguett. In it, the male dancer is dressed as a tough Parisian street type, the woman as his 'moll'. The dance, which enjoyed a lasting popularity, involved the man generally mistreating his unfortunate partner, throwing her around the stage in a variety of dangerously athletic moves. Mistinguett called it 'an alternation between caresses and struggles, brutality and sensual tenderness'.

about her affection for the young dancer that she had plucked out of the chorus, a chorus that included, amongst others, a curvaceous blonde destined years later to become world-famous – Mae West.

The show itself did good business, despite a very poor *Variety* review that criticised everything in it apart from Al Jolson. *Variety* was never able to give Gaby good reviews. The bad feelings between her and the most widely read and influential show business publication in the United States originated from the time of her 'Why I take all I can and give nothing back' statement to the *New York Journal*. Coincidentally Alan Dale, the author of the condemnatory article in that publication to which Gaby was replying, also wrote a regular column for *Variety*.

Vera Violetta ran on over the Christmas holidays. Gaby's contract with the Shuberts for this trip expired early in the New Year and she started planning her return to Europe. She had been corresponding with Alfred Moul, who was eager to re-book her for the following winter season. Many managements in Europe were equally as keen to employ her, and she had become adept at pitting one against the other, a tactic Charlot had noted and warned Moul about earlier in the year. Now she did at least promise Moul that she would not discuss work with anyone else in London, but at the same time let it be known that she was being courted constantly by the Palace Theatre, which, under Alfred Butt's management had gained much prestige, and was the Alhambra's closest rival in London.

Moul had agreed to pay her £325 per week – more than triple the amount that music-hall top-liners like George Robey were being paid. This salary would include two matinées. When Gaby sent the contract back from New York, she had amended it to read that she would receive £325, whether she performed matinées or not. Alfred Moul saw red. He wrote to her: 'I am compelled to inform you that the question of your engagement is now abandoned by the Alhambra management.' Knowing that she would be welcomed with open arms at the Palace, Gaby was not dismayed.

Her depature from New York was as sensational as her arrival. She took with her thousands of dollars, a black maid, a baby crocodile, and, to the great chagrin of the Shuberts, Harry Pilcer.

8

NO HONEYMOON

Gaby's reception back home in France bordered on hysteria. She and Harry Pilcer were photographed, interviewed, followed; not a day went by without some item about them appearing in the press. Rumours about their friendship abounded, and Gaby had to deny time and time again that they had been married. Harry took to his new-found celebrity like a duck to water, assisting Gaby at her press conferences, and escorting her everywhere. She was certainly in love with him, and it seemed to be reciprocal.

Under Harry's guidance, Gaby's dancing had improved out of all recognition, gaining rapidly in pace and style, and the combination of their talents on stage was explosive. As well as the 'Gaby Glide,' they introduced the 'Grizzly Bear', and their style was soon being copied by a host of imitators.

Gaby's version of her American tour, as told to the European press, naturally enough concentrated on the glories, though she was quick to point out that she had been far from dazzled by it all. 'Everything is big there – houses, businesses, theatres – but the bluff is the biggest thing of all,' she said. She recounted the dramatic details of their return journey. The black maid had fallen overboard and drowned. Even her pet crocodile had not survived the journey: when the customs men opened its cage, it was dead. Her life, as related to the press, contained only sensation and glamour. No hint of the extraordinary financial wrangling that preceded her performances, nor of her feud with Jolson, ever reached European ears. But, with regard to Harry Pilcer, the *Tatler*'s witty and anonymous correspondent in Paris, who called herself Priscilla, wrote: 'What did you think of the rumour that Gaby Deslys had married an American dancer? No one believed it over here; we all know how practical young Gaby is . . .'

Once settled in Paris, Gaby applied herself to her normal

hard-working routine and on 2 February 1912, the tiny auditorium of the Fémina Theatre on the Champs Elysées was packed for her first European appearance since the American tour. The dance routines Harry had worked out for them whipped the crowd into a frenzy of enthusiasm. They cheered wildly as Harry whisked her round, hoisted her above his head, and threw her about the stage in a series of crazy contortions, all performed to the latest ragtime rhythms. One number, 'Come and Dance', had to be repeated three times before the audience was satisfied.

When she was not rehearsing or being fitted for increasingly revealing outfits, Gaby was with her agents, lawyers, financial advisers and press agents. Organizing her career was as demanding as running a thriving business; she was living her life at five hundred miles an hour, ever haunted by the spectre of that aged actress. While her sun was shining, she determined to make so much hay the cart would collapse under the strain. That is, if she did not do so first.

Her mother worried about her continually, and would have liked her to spend a little time resting in Paris, but nothing could subdue Gaby's formidable energy. Maman was at least grateful that her other daughter was not as driven. Matichon had a moderately successful career as Kerville, and, thanks to Gaby's contacts, was employed as frequently as she wanted to be. She had played regularly at the Folies-Bergère, and had recently enjoyed a season at the Olympia. Although she did not share Gaby's theatrical ambitions, she had developed a similar taste for the good things in life. At some point, she hoped that she would meet a man rich enough to supply her with them. When that happened, she would willingly retire from the stage. In the meantime, she was happy to live with Maman in Gaby's Paris house, and to bide her time.

Gaby rushed to London for a few days to arrange a winter contract. Alfred Moul had regretted his earlier decision, and tried to get her back to the Alhambra, but was too late. Alfred Butt had already signed her for the Palace at an undisclosed sum, but one which was rumoured to be the largest ever paid to a variety artist on the London stage. With this contract tucked firmly under her belt, she rushed back to Paris to prepare for a short season in Vienna. Before going there, she found time to pose for the photographer

Reutlinger.* The results of this session were daring in the extreme, including one shot of Gaby in her dressingroom having her garters adjusted by her maid, which was reproduced all over the world.

Another short season in Paris followed that in Vienna, and, in July she gave a fabulous fête at the Fémina Theatre. It took the form of a dancing competition, and started at midnight so that as many performers as possible could take part after their shows had finished. It was an evening of great excitement, with couples doing the 'Grizzly Bear', the 'Bunny Hug', and, most popular of all, a new craze called the 'Tango'. This sad and sensual dance had originated in the brothels of Buenos Aires, and had after some years reached Paris. The guests all tried to outdo each other in the splendour of their costumes. The rash of Orientalism that would eventually spread over the fashionable world in the wake of the *Ballets Russes* had already gripped Paris, and was much in evidence that night. The small Fémina Theatre was a seething kaleidoscope of brilliantly coloured and diaphanous chiffons, rich brocades and velvets, generously cut into harem pants, tunics and turbans, with every imaginable type of bead, sequin and spangle flashing in the spotlights, as the dancers swayed to rhythms as exotic and exciting as their dress.

Gaby and Harry had planned the whole thing together, and she was thrilled with the success of their collaboration. For the first time, she had a partner to plan things with and, to an extent, some of the burden of her professional life had been lifted. With Harry's brilliant dance routines, the whole character of her act changed: Harry's slick, modern choreography, which in no way detracted from Gaby's personal attractions, took the emphasis off her singing. This was a good thing, as her voice got weaker every time her throat was ravaged by recurrent infections. Having a stage partner also added a new dimension to her sexuality: the dances that Harry worked out involved all kinds of contact between them, from soft romantic smooches, to the wild excesses of the 'Gaby Glide'.

Gaby had never performed such a wide variety of steps. Under Harry's tuition, her dancing transcended the mediocre and became great. Slicker and more self-assured, she held her audience with an

* Sister of the distinguished actress Cécile Sorel.

authority which she had not possessed before, but which she had observed in professionals like Al Jolson. She was able to display all her new expertise that winter at her new home – the Palace Theatre in London.

The Palace had been managed, towards the end of his life, by 'the father of the halls', Charles Morton, who had turned it from a commercial failure into an important variety theatre. On Morton's death in 1904, Alfred Butt had taken over, and under him its prestige increased enormously. Maud Allan had caused a sensation there with her barefoot, bare-legged dancing, and the incandescent beauty of Anna Pavlova had more recently been delighting the crowds. Alfred Butt's achievements had been crowned the previous year when, on 1 July 1912, King George V had attended the first Royal Variety Command Performance in this theatre.

Alfred Butt realized that whatever he paid Gaby at this high point of her career would be worth it. Since the Manuel scandal had died down, her public image had acquired an innocent yet provocative gallic charm that was still all the rage in London. People coming to see her expected something saucy. If she had had love affairs with famous figures, it added to the spice of her appearance, but the last thing people in England wanted was the fine details. Even the idea of having a picture of King Manuel on the set, as *Variety* had suggested, would, in England, have been considered tasteless in the extreme. One of the reasons for Gaby's continued success in London was the fact that, although alluring, even sexy, her performance to date had just about remained within the confines of good taste. However, after the inclusion of Harry in her routines, this was thought by many to be no longer the case.

Photographs published in England before her much-heralded appearance at the Palace, show Gaby entwined with Harry in various dance routines. Her eyes smile into his, his arms are around her waist, her little bejewelled hands caress his face. '*Not* married – Mlle Deslys and friend' was typical of the captions accompanying these pictures in the press. Other photographs from this same session were released in France, but were totally unsuitable for publication in England. They were of an extremely erotic nature. In one, the culmination of an 'Apache'-style dance, Harry lies on the floor in a submissive pose, with Gaby crouched over him. His shirt is ripped into tatters, revealing a good deal of his torso. In another, he is bent backwards over a chair in the torn shirt; Gaby, in a short skirt slashed almost to the waist, bends over him; their bodies are pressed together. It remains erotic even in 1986. In the England of 1912 it was unprintable.

This kind of publicity, together with her stage act, was beginning to cause some comment, even in the more liberal moral climate of France. On 21 June 1912, the theatrical writer and critic Ernest Charles, published a lengthy article in *Gil Blas* deploring the decline of moral standards in the music hall. He claimed that many artists offered the public entertainment of a cheap and debasing nature, and cited Gaby Deslys to illustrate his point. In a blistering personal attack on her, he stated that he found her devoid of any talent and opined that her whole theatrical success was due to explicit sexuality.

That same day Gaby informed *Gil Blas* and Ernest Charles that she would sue them for 50,000 francs for defamation. The next day, in *Gil Blas*, Charles announced this forthcoming action, reiterated his opinions about Gaby, and said he was grateful to her for giving him the opportunity of furthering his campaign to clean up the music halls by bringing the whole issue into the courts. Following the second article, Gaby announced that she would sue him twice, and in a public statement said that, irrespective of Monsieur Charles' personal opinions, she and the music hall managers were only giving the public what they wanted. Although she eventually lost her case, she gained tremendous support both from the public and from members of her profession. And of course, it made good copy.

News of this business reached London, and Alfred Butt advertized the forthcoming appearance of the controversial star widely. By the time she arrived, the British public was expecting something special. The whole revue, of which Gaby had the star turn, was of the highest quality. Unlike the Shubert Brothers, Alfred Butt surrounded his star with beauty and talent; she was a pearl set in diamonds. And there was no Jolson to detract from her confidence or her personality.

Her sketch, called *Mademoiselle Chic*, dealt 'in a very open manner' with the dilemma of a *demimondaine* who tries to choose between love and money. In other words, it provided an excuse for Gaby to appear in all sorts of unlikely and breathtaking costumes, including one consisting of a modified tutu with layers of tulle, a plunging neckline, and a headdress festooned with cherries. On her back fluttered dozens of tulle wings. This enchanting fairy made, amongst other things, the cover of the *Sketch*, Britain's best-selling weekly.

The bedroom scene originating from *Chichine*, which was destined to become a standard feature of revues for decades to come, was repeated. Once again, Gaby was seen leaping in and out of bed in a variety of unlikely nightgowns. The scene that caused the most discussion involved her actually stripping off her evening gown whilst on stage, and cavorting around in her underwear. Although disrobing acts had been performed twelve years earlier at the Paris Exhibition and, indeed, five years prior to that at the Olympia, on both occasions by Louise Willy, it was the first time that a big international star had incorporated such an element into her act. Although the turn was modest by today's standards, underwear of the time being considerably more substantial than now, some sections of the public were shocked, and would have been more so, had not Gaby performed with such lightheartedness and wit. 'Very alluring, very *insouciante*, and . . . really rather funny . . . leaving no moral taint behind,' as one reviewer in the *Tatler* said.

Whether Gaby was alluring, *insouciante*, or simply shocking, was after all a question of personal taste. Her genteel strip in *Mademoiselle Chic* was in fact quite tame compared to some of the sights on offer in Paris, where, despite the efforts of would-be reformers like Ernest Charles, the first bare breasts had already been fleetingly glimpsed at the Folies-Bergère. But what went on in Paris would not necessarily pass in London. West-End audiences going to see Parisian performers expected to see something spicy but, nevertheless, Gaby caused a few rumblings in the more conservative sections of society. There was even talk of complaints being received by the Lord Chamberlain. It would be a while, however, before these rumblings developed into a full-scale quake.

Not surprisingly, audiences at the Palace consisted mostly of men. The big Palace bar was one of its main attractions. Staffed by a large team of barmaids, carefully chosen for their buxom figures and cheery personalities, evenings passed when some patrons got no further. It was miraculous how the bar emptied when Gaby Deslys came on stage; crowds of men in black evening dress jostled each other in the crammed standing room at the back of the auditorium to catch a glimpse of the tiny figure, her fragile, blonde, elfin presence holding them in its spell.

Every night the stage door would be crowded with admirers: elderly businessmen, toffs in top hats, young men-about-town, and a growing number of women, for young working-class women admired her tremendously. The chambermaids and shop girls saw in her something to aspire to; saw how she had clawed her way up from obscure beginnings to become one of the world's most glamorous figures, and it gave them hope. Her jewels, her furs, her cars, her royal lovers had become legendary. She was a popular topic of conversation and gossip in kitchens, sculleries and drawing rooms. Upstairs and down, every detail of her life, as weekly chronicled in the *Tatler* and *Sketch*, was dissected and analyzed.

Although Gaby was the subject of some censure with the older, more staid members of society, the young of all classes adored her. Nightly they competed with their parents' generation for seats in the vast auditorium, packing the gallery and stalls to view their heroine. She was more loved in London than anywhere else. In America her publicity had not always been favourable, but English critics and audiences were willing to take her at face value. She did not have the voice of Tetrazzini, but she certainly had her own brand of glamour, and as far as her act was concerned, the gorgeous and increasingly outrageous costumes, fabulous jewels and, now, thanks to Harry Pilcer, brilliant dancing, made her a major attraction.

She and Harry had been together for over a year and during that time they were inseparable. Communication had not always been easy, but it was improving. Harry said later that in this early period he had to explain dance routines to Gaby with his feet, as she found his American accent incomprehensible, and he spoke no French. There were other difficulties with their relationship: both had strong personalities so their ideas would sometimes clash. Gaby had been used to running her act her own way and, although she was always willing to be guided by Harry's expertise in dance, she did not gladly take his advice on other aspects of her act. Loud disagreements backstage were often the result. But they always made up, and on stage they continued to be a magical combination. The 'Gaby Glide' caused a furore.

Gaby had hoped to be able to have a little free time to prepare herself for her second American season that winter, but Alfred Butt pleaded with her to play a few more weeks, as business was so good, and so they stayed on well into the autumn.

It was not only the Palace that was making money out of her. Gaby had been parodied constantly since the Manuel affair and it seemed that no revue was complete without an impersonation of her. During 1912, May Flower had 'done' her at the Alhambra in *The Guide to Paris*; there was a skit in the enormously successful George Grossmith revue, *Kill that Fly*; and a hilarious and clever send-up of Deslys and Pilcer in *Everybody's Doing It* at the Empire, with Ida Crispi as Gaby teaching Robert Hale, as Sir Francis Drake, how to do her 'Glide'. Believing imitation to be the sincerest form of flattery, Gaby loved it.

She had announced earlier in the year that she intended to build a theatre for herself, where she could present her own revues. By now other artists, from Réjane to Bernhardt, and in America Julian Eltinge, the world's most famous drag artist, had their own showplaces. She planned, as ever, something big – 'not a little machine' – with over two thousand seats. Designed along American lines, it would be an innovation in Europe. She had signed a further contract with the Shuberts to tour the United States from coast to coast before ending up in the Winter Garden in February of 1913 for the spring revue there, and considered that with the $20,000 a month she would be earning, the theatre could be built by the end of 1914. She also claimed to have two very wealthy – and anonymous – admirers, one in America and one in London, who would be willing to back her with further funds.

Gaby boarded the *Caronia* at Liverpool on 2 November 1912, bound for New York. Any fear she had of crossing the ocean was now forgotten. The journey was uneventful apart from an incident about halfway across the Atlantic, when a sailor named Jerry Shea fell from the crow's nest, breaking an arm and several ribs. On hearing of the accident, Gaby personally made a collection for his family. She received sufficient funds to keep them off the breadline while he recovered.

On arrival in New York, she descended the gangplank in an electric blue gown and black coat, both trimmed with chinchilla. Before leaving London, she had acquired two tiny marmosets named Alfonse and Chichine, and with these in her arms, and with Harry at her side (in a bright yellow suit and carrying a teddy bear), she faced the battery of waiting reporters. They all wanted to know about 'the wedding'.

'What wedding?' asked Gaby.

'You and Harry, of course,' someone informed her, and added, 'Don't you read the papers?'

This brought forth raucous laughter from the gang of reporters, but Gaby was not amused.

'Which papers? Show me,' she demanded, and one of the morning's editions was produced for her inspection. The front page carried a picture of her and Harry with the headline, 'Gaby and Harry Wed', followed by the report of a statement issued in Paris by Madame Caire, in which she said that she had received a cable from her daughter saying, 'Was married to Harry this morning, very happy'. Poor Maman had been unable to verify the story with her daughter, for Gaby had been halfway across the Atlantic, and she had not, in fact, doubted the authenticity of the cable that had been sent to her.

Gaby was furious at this hoax, but for more complicated reasons than were at first apparent. She was upset that Maman had been duped; and also because persistent rumours of her marriage were becoming a sore point with her. The truth was that she was only too eager to become Harry's wife, but he had never proposed. She had even suggested to him that they get married, but to her surprise, he had turned her down. Their physical relationship had been slow in starting; one of the reasons she found him so attractive was that he had not tried to get her into bed within five minutes of their meeting. Nor within five days, nor even five weeks. She intimated in interviews given in Paris when they first returned from New York that they had finally become lovers on the boat over, but that seemed a long time ago. Their relationship continued, but marriage was a subject that Harry never brought up. 'Well, we are not married. Please tell everybody that this is not true,' she stormed at the reporters, before charging off to the customs hall with Harry and his teddy bear trailing behind.

The customs hall proved to be another ordeal in a long trip that would hold many far worse ones for her. A customs official told her that her trunks – all twenty-six of them – would have to go to the public stores for further examination, leaving her stamping her feet with rage. When she had made out her customs declaration on the ship before arriving in port, she had stated that her jewels, mostly pearls, were worth $325,000 including a necklace of sapphires and diamonds worth $40,000; she carried a diamond collar ($40,000), one collar of forty-one matched white pearls ($40,000), one of forty-three pearls ($36,000), another of eighty-seven smaller pearls ($27,000), another pearl necklace ($51,000), a diamond pendant with seven stones ($18,000), two solitaire pearl rings ($13,000 and $15,200), and a diamond tiara ($16,000). The gowns she valued at $50,000.

The customs appraiser, on looking at the gems, thought these sums were too high, but the newspapers the following day were full of the news that they had been officially appraised at around these same figures. It is difficult to judge what these gems would be worth today. Pearls have only recently become fashionable again, but rows of large, matched Oriental pearls are exceedingly rare, as are the huge solitaires Gaby favoured for rings. To obtain some idea of the current value of her jewellery, one could easily substitute pound signs for the dollars and multiply by five. Gaby had by this time become extremely knowledgeable about gem stones, pearls in particular, and only the best would do. One will never be able to say for certain where she acquired them, but the very long string of fat pearls she was photographed in from around 1909 was supposed to have come from King Manuel, and would today be priceless. Of course, all this publicity about the value of her jewellery made her the target of several unsuccessful robbery attempts. Only once did thieves make off with some of her best pearls, but she had had the foresight to have copies made, and they only got away with fakes.

73

The whole trip was dogged by bad luck and worse publicity. She had further trouble with Al Jolson. To her dismay, the Shuberts had arranged for her to join Jolson on the road in a revue called *The Social Whirl*, and she opened in this at the Lyric, Philadelphia, in December 1912. Once again, Jolson's antipathy towards her manifested itself very quickly; soon he was up to all his old tricks, doing his best to humiliate her whilst they were on stage together and generally detract from her performance. He was furious that she was billed above him and, at $5000 per week, was earning far more. Indeed, the only peformer whose salary approached this figure at the time was Sarah Bernhardt★, who was also currently touring the United States, but even so, the $7000 per week she was being paid was for her entire company; Gaby's $5000 was for her alone. Having her own train was another distinction Gaby shared with the 'Divine Sarah'; between stops the company travelled on the *Gaby Special*.

The Social Whirl took big money everywhere it was performed, and the brief tour took in Boston, Montreal and Buffalo, averaging a weekly take of over $20,000. The troupe disbanded early in 1913, so rehearsals could start for the big new revue at the Winter Garden, which opened in February. Called *The Honeymoon Express*, this was a lavish production, notable for its cast, which, as well as Gaby and Harry, Jolson, Harry Fox and Jenny Dolly (of the Dolly Sisters), included a brilliant young singing comedienne called Fanny Brice in one of her first featured roles.

The show was a masterpiece of staging. In the most memorable sequence, the express train which gave the show its name was seen racing with a fast car, its headlights in the distance becoming brighter and brighter until, with incredible light and sound effects, they appeared to burst into the audience. It was a smash hit, taking over $30,000 at the box office in the first week, and averaging $28,000 for some time after that. Gaby's

★ Curious though it may be to envisage the world's greatest actress as a variety turn, that is in fact what she was at this point in her career. Of course, the programme would be on a much more highbrow level than the average touring show, and she did herself have the final say as to who would share her bill. On her winter 1913 tour of the United States, she drew the line at a troupe of acrobats, and they had to be taken off before she would continue.

personal reviews were very mixed. *Variety* called her 'vulgar' for not wearing tights beneath her 'extremely light under-dressing', revealed when Harry tore off her skirt in the inevitable bedroom scene. The Puritan streak in American culture was still, evidently, quite strong.

Her reputation as a *femme fatale* was furthered by numerous stories about men who had lost their hearts and apparently, their heads over her. One of these, widely circulated around the Christmas of 1912, involved a very wealthy Wall Street broker, who on several occasions attempted to secure an introduction to her. He wrote to her many times, crazed fan letters of a type she was used to getting, but when she received one that said, 'unless you see me I shall do something desperate', she agreed to meet him. He appeared at her dressing room the next night, told her he was totally in love with her, and proposed there and then that they should get married. When she tried to reason with him, he rushed out into the street and shot himself. Unlikely though it may seem, this story was sufficiently widely publicized for one to suspect that there may have been some truth in it. It was not the kind of story Gaby would have wanted people to believe, but she published no denial of it.

It is incredible that, rather than dissuade wealthy admirers, Gaby's reputation as a man-eater seemed to spur them on to new heights of generosity. She had publicly stated that she was not prepared to meet just anybody, no matter how wealthy they were, and consequently her company became the ultimate status symbol amongst the richest men-about-town. Wherever she went, millionaires clamoured to pay her court and lavish gifts on her. These ranged from the simply costly to the bizarre. Knowing her fondness for animals, someone even sent her a baby elephant. After posing with it for photographs, she sold it to Buffalo Bill's menagerie.

She was, by the spring of 1913, becoming homesick. Maman had visited her in March, when Gaby gave a big party at the Plaza to introduce her to eighteen or so members of the cast, but now she wanted to go home. All the money she was making could not compensate for the extraordinary and public life that went with it. She longed to be back in Europe, missed her little house in Paris, yearned to be back in London where audiences adored her, and where they wrote nice things about her in the papers. She was relieved when her contract for the trip came to an end in April 1913; she had had enough. On 27 April she gave a pretty little farewell speech after the curtain call, saying how sorry she was to be leaving. Some of the audience may even have believed it.

9

A QUESTION OF DECENCY

In the fashionable world of 1913, the catastrophic war that was to wipe out an entire generation of young men, and irrevocably change the role of women, was as yet unpresaged.

Fashion, not only in dress but also in most aspects of social behaviour, had changed profoundly in the years since the death of Queen Victoria. The basic structure of society remained unchanged, but to be young and even only fairly well-off was a far more amusing and colourful experience than it had been a decade earlier. The most fashionable and avant-garde young women were shedding their corsets, painting their faces, smoking and drinking, and all without ruining their reputations, although it would be a few years before all this could be considered normal behaviour for a well-bred 'gel'.

The theatre and society were inextricably connected, and it became almost respectable to embark on a stage career. 'Gaps left by actresses marrying into the aristocracy filled by aristocracy becoming wedded to the stage', was the caption accompanying a picture in *Tatler* of the latest society actress, Mrs George Lindsay. So, as Lily Elsie settled down as the wife of a Scottish laird in her castle in Perthshire, Lady Constance Stewart-Richardson prepared to do her barefoot dances on Broadway. It was indeed a crazy world, filled with ever more giddy and bizarrely dressed young people.

The huge sensation created in 1909 by Sergei Diaghilev's Russian Ballet had proved a lasting one. Nijinsky, Karsavina and Pavlova had become established as the world's foremost dancers, and the romantic Near East of Bakst's costume designs had caused the borders of popular taste to be pushed even further towards the Orient. The stages of the West End became crowded with exotic foreign dancers. India was represented by Sahari Djeli and Roshanara, and on the Continent numerous imports included a very unusual Courtesan and Oriental dancer named Mata Hari ('Eye of the Day'), who was a Dutch girl called Margarete Zelle, and who was later discovered to have spied for both France and Germany during the First World War.

The Far East was further evoked by successful productions of *Turandot, The Mikado* and a rash of plays with biblical themes. It was not long before the passion for Oriental costume descended from the stage to everyday life, at least for the rich. In Paris, Paul Poiret had been throwing a series of lavish and well-publicized costume balls, and the vogue for these soon crossed the Channel. Before long, fashionable salons and ballrooms in London began to resemble a colossal pantomime; gentleman with blackened faces, turbans and gold sashes accompanying ladies who were hybrids of Salome, Madam Butterfly and Mary Magdalene. To the jerky rhythms of ragtime, frenzied couples did the 'Turkey Trot', the 'Russian Ramp' and dozens of other extraordinary and ridiculous dances; new fads rapidly replacing old ones, that had barely taken off, each more ungainly than the last. *Punch* remarked unkindly: 'We now hear that the freak dances that have made their appearance in our ballrooms have been the vogue for many years in our lunatic asylums.'

When the 'Tango' finally appeared in England in the spring of 1913, everything else became out-dated. Before long, 'Tango Teas' were being held everywhere, and society mothers were questioning the safety of their daughters at such functions, where crowds of strangely garbed and painted young people moved in a fug of cigarette smoke to the sensual Latin rhythms.

The hobble skirt, which had first made its appearance around 1911, had by this time become so exaggeratedly tight-fitting that 'the unfortunate wearer was unable to walk, stoop or climb, much less run, with any comfort', according to the *Sketch*. The paper recorded that, 'the ladies are reduced to a kind of Chinese toddle and some of them resemble nothing as much as competitors in a sack race who, once they have fallen, are unable to get up. Parisians appropriately call the wearers of these skirts *"les entravées"*, the shackled ones'.

The long strides of the 'Tango' required that modifications be made, so the victims of fashion opened their impossible skirts at the front, revealing tantalizing stretches of ankle and calf, even knees. The more fashionable they were, the more leg they showed. To balance this revelation at the lower half of the body, many designers decreed, at least for evening wear, V-necks, and deep V-backs. One contemporary wag remarked that the only part of the body it was not decent to show was the ears, still covered by long hair pulled down from a centre parting into a chignon or pleat, *à la* Cléo de Mérode.

All of Gaby Deslys' stage clothes were exaggerated adaptations of current styles, and fashion's wild extravagances in this final year before the war found full expression in the extraordinary costumes she was preparing for her next show at the Palace – *A la Carte*. Described in voluminous pre-show publicity as being 'the very latest creations of Parisian *modistes*', these costumes were not typical of the work of Maison Paquin, who had made most of them to the design of Etienne Drian. Landolff, famous for his stage costumes, had also designed a few. One can also be sure that Gaby herself contributed a great deal; every outfit had a bizarre beauty that bore her personal stamp. As Cecil Beaton put it, 'She walked the tightrope of a near-barbarous taste with a rare audacity, scarcely regarding the drop to utter vulgarity below her'.

Each costume was unique; each one a more outrageous exaggeration of fashion than the last. The tightest possible hobble skirts were swathed around her hips, slit to reveal a flash of leg, then trailed off into a tasselled fishtail dragging a couple of feet behind her. These dresses were not made for dancing; even walking was difficult. They were made for posing. Gaby would totter onto the stage, staying only long enough to sing a song, or to exchange a little witty dialogue with Harry Pilcer, who then held the stage with a virtuoso dance routine while she went off to change once again. No one knew what she would come back in – 'or if she would come back in anything at all' (*Tatler*). She sometimes executed her own dance routines in the widest, sheerest harem pants, topped with a short, circular lampshade skirt of the type associated with Paul Poiret. These costumes excited the men in the audience to a fever pitch; the fashionable ladies to ecstasies of envy.

It had been a year since her last London performance. She had gone directly from America into rehearsals in Paris for a modified version of *The Honeymoon Express* at the Paris Alhambra, and had followed this with a brief rest. It had been months since she had been ill, she was even beginning to hope that she had once and for all kicked the throat weakness that had dogged her for so long. She relished the thought of appearing once again at the Palace before her favourite London audiences.

Manuel was finally out of her life for good. His mother had eventually found him an acceptable bride, Princess Augustine Victoria of Hohenzollern. Gaby smiled wryly to herself when she saw the wedding pictures in the papers: the Princess bore a startling resemblance to her. Some of the illustrated weeklies wickedly carried pictures of the happy royal couple on one page, shots of Gaby in her new *A la Carte* costumes opposite. Her amusement must also have been tinged with sadness. If she did have an intimate relationship with Manuel, as she claimed, it had been a rare occurrence in a life preoccupied with work. Her true feelings towards him remain obscure, and it will probably now never be known whether she regarded him merely as a stepping stone to international fame, or as one of the great romantic attachments of her life. The truth probably lies somewhere between the two. In either case, she must have felt regret at seeing him pass from her life.

Alfred Butt made sure no one could miss the fact that Gaby was back. A huge cut-out figure of her lying down, resting her chin on her hand, was hoisted up on the façade of the immense Palace building at Cambridge Circus. 'She's back!' declared letters ten feet high above it. From the minute she arrived to begin rehearsals in September, the whole of London knew of her presence. If they had not read the papers, they could hardly miss hearing about or even catching sight of the electric brougham, that most modish form of transport, that ferried her around the West End, and stood waiting for her each night outside the stage door on Shaftesbury Avenue.

A youthful Douglas Byng recalls seeing this conveyance, 'with its canework body, and huge Old English sheepdog seated up front next to the driver'. Cries of 'Look, it's Gaby!' would accompany its stately progress to and from the Palace Theatre, her little blonde figure in the back smiling and waving for her fans like royalty. Cecil Beaton wrote: 'As she drove off, people would see her sitting framed in the window, creating an effect comparable to the passing of the Queen of Sheba'.

The plot of *A la Carte* was of little consequence: it was Gaby, Harry, her costumes and their dance that people wanted to see. The wild convolutions of the 'Gaby Glide' were exaggerated even further by Harry. In fact, some of the choreography was downright dangerous. One of the sets was a huge staircase,* up and down which he and Gaby would dance with frenzied contortions, descending, at one point, with Gaby's legs wrapped around her partner's waist.

The costumes caused more than a sensation, they caused a national scandal. The rumblings that had been heard the previous year, the questions asked by certain factions as to the decency of her act, got louder and louder, and finally erupted. A representative of the Bishop of Kensington went to the Palace, witnessed the performance, and was deeply shocked. The Bishop lost no time in writing a letter of complaint to the Lord Chamberlain, claiming that in parts *A La Carte* was 'grossly indecent'. The Lord Chamberlain in turn wrote a letter to Alfred Butt, stating, 'If Public Morality be any further outraged at the Palace Theatre, the piece in question will be immediately forbidden and your licence for plays will be cancelled'.

Alfred Butt was incensed. His reply, published in *The Times* on 23 October 1913, stated that he 'had been very careful, since the Lord Chamberlain had received certain complaints the previous year, to ensure that there should be nothing whatsoever in the script or the interpretation thereof to which anyone could possibly take exception, and I am quite satisfied that any performance given here is far more decent and free from suggestion than many

---

* This staircase set was widely copied, and eventually became a standard feature of spectacular revues.

81

performances given nightly elsewhere in London'. What, then, was all the fuss about? The 'Gaby Glide' was certainly not graceful, but was it indecent? Surely not, said Mr Butt. The scene where she powders her legs? High spirited tomfoolery; she was even wearing flesh-coloured stockings! So what? he asked.

The answer, of course, was not *what* was being done, but *who* was doing it. Alfred Butt suggested that the Bishop's implication was that Gaby Deslys was an immoral woman, and therefore that anything she did on stage constituted a display of immorality. She was evidently being condemned on the strength of her notoriety, and the injustice of this did not go unremarked. As a result the whole issue of public morality and the music halls came into open discussion. The argument boiled fast and furious for weeks. Was she indecent or was she not? The Bishop certainly thought so; many others did not.

One of the most illustrious defenders of Gaby's good name was George Bernard Shaw. Although he would not pass judgement on her, he questioned the right of the Church to do so. In the first of a series of long letters to *The Times*, he pointed out the difficulty of deciding what endangered public morals, and what did not. He indicated that, as far as the Bishop was concerned, 'He is assuming that what he approves of is right, and what he disapproves of wrong . . . He will have to admit that his epithet of "objectionable", merely means "disliked by the Bishop of Kensington".' As far as deciding in the long run what offended the public and what did not, Shaw considered that, 'Miss Gaby Deslys is as much entitled to the benefit of the doubt as is the Bishop'. A long and bitter exchange between the playwright and the Bishop ensued, with various other notables, including H. B. Irving, joining the fray.

Gaby defended herself in a rather poignant open letter, stating that she did nothing on stage that acrobats and dancers the whole world over did not do all the time. In substance, of course, she was right. But other dancers and acrobats did not enjoy her lurid off-stage reputation. One reader even wrote to *The Times* that, 'The objection alleged against Mlle Deslys' performances was that it is suggestive, not of sexual emotion, but of vice, or the corruption of sexual emotion'.

Gaby made a good pretence of being horrified. Backstage at the Palace, she gave an interview to the *Evening News* seated in her dressing room, surrounded by banks of lilies, a blue chiffon peignoir trimmed with white marabou belted loosely around her waist. As she talked, Chichine, her little marmoset, clambered on and off his mistress' lap, rattling around the pots of make-up and ropes of pearls littering her dressing table. Gaby became very eloquent on the subject of the Church and the stage. 'Do you know,' she said, 'that although a lot of foolish people think that my dresses are almost improper, I am really a very religious girl? I am not only good, but pious.' As she said this the marmoset fell into a large pot of rouge, apparently from shock. Gaby burst into laughter, calling her maid to clean up the mess.

She may indeed have been hurt at being called 'grossly indecent', but despite her protestations, she was privately thrilled by the publicity. Public opinion was largely on her side, and George Bernard Shaw pointed out that, despite the Bishop finding *A la Carte* objectionable, 'this entertainment . . . has proved highly attractive to large numbers of people whose taste is entitled to the same consideration as his own'. Mr Butt refused to change or modify any detail of the sketch, and the large hall was crammed to absolute capacity night after night as people came to make up their own minds.

A young Osbert Sitwell came one night. Far from being offended, he was enchanted:

'. . . in her brief songs, dances and scraps of acting and conversation, all of which she entered up and executed with a sort of casual deliberateness, she was curiously effective. There was no one to approach her in her own form of stage glamour, and strange, yet banal, allurement. To a flourish of elementary ragtime, very French in its accent, on the part of the theatre orchestra – usually to the "Gaby Glide", a tune possessed of a peculiarly inappropriate and naive gaiety – she would come from the wings in a flutter of silk, feathers, flesh and jewels, drenched in light, and the star would have arrived to join her partner, Harry Pilcer, who, by a convention, would already be looking for her ("Where can she be? Where is she?"). The moment that she was there, rather heavy shouldered for her body, and crested like a bird, for she was wearing on her head a tight-fitting cap loaded with ostrich feathers, she seemed with her fair hair and tawny, fair skin, to absorb every ray of light in the theatre, to exist only in that flaring, sputtering brightness of another world, to be outlined with the icy fires of a diamond. She would sing a little, dance for a moment, as if she was almost too fragile, and too much in need of protection, to execute the steps, sing in her voice with the rolling Rs of her French throat, unmusical but provocative, and the whole result was perfect of its kind, a work of art, but specialized as the courtship dance of a bird, with the same glittering and drumming vanity, except that here the female and not the male played the chief role.'*

As Gaby played the dominant role with Harry on stage, so she did in their private life. She had been an established star when they met, and Harry had been an unknown. She had boosted his career in much the same way as King Manuel had boosted hers. It was due to her initiative that they had become dance partners, and eventually lovers. It was also Gaby who had broached the subject of marriage many times in the two and a half years since they had met, but Harry remained unresponsive. By now, she may have begun to suspect that, intimate though their friendship might be, and great though their stage partnership undoubtedly was, this was not the totally committed romance that had been missing from her life. Harry was unable, or unwilling, to fulfil that rôle. If he was not yet known in theatrical circles to be gay, he certainly would be so later on. However, whatever the exact nature of their relationship may have been, they retained a close, if increasingly volatile friendship.

Gaby, meantime, had become chic. She was the darling of a new young society eager to shake off the restricting shackles of Victorianism. As far as they were concerned, the Bishops signified the nineteenth century and Gaby was very much of the twentieth: a woman for today, independent and free, unrestricted by corsetry and old-fashioned moral standards; her nightly performance at the Palace a statement of modernism. Gaby had caused the whole issue of public morality to be called into question, and in the final analysis

* Extract from *Great Morning* by Osbert Sitwell.

can be seen to have done a great deal towards liberating the theatre
from the fetters of a system of censorship long outdated.

George Bernard Shaw was not the only famous playwright who
was aware of Gaby's existence. One night, Alfred Butt knocked on
the door of the star dressing room. Pulling on her peignoir, Gaby
asked her maid to see who it was. Mr Butt entered, followed by a
man whose face Gaby recognized instantly. 'Gaby,' said Sir Alfred,
'I'd like you to meet an old friend of mine. Mademoiselle Deslys,
Sir James Barrie.'

With this introduction, Gaby embarked on one of the most
puzzling and intriguing relationships of her life. She immediately
liked the shy Scotsman who kissed her hand so decorously, his sad,
pale eyes meeting hers in undisguised admiration. He immediately
told her how enchanting he found her, how delighted he had been
by her performance that night. They fell into easy conversation, but
when he suddenly and without warning said he would like to give
her a chinchilla coat, Gaby hardly knew what to say. She guessed
that he must have heard how much she liked receiving gifts, but it
was a bizarre gesture nonetheless.

After securing her promise to lunch with him and Alfred Butt the
next day, her distinguished visitor left, leaving Gaby rather
bewildered. She was not beyond feeling flattered. Although used
to the attentions of aristocratic, even sovereign, playboys, Barrie
was theatrical royalty, and the artiste as well as the woman
felt honoured. At their next meeting she did not, however,
look remotely like a commoner at court. As they stood on the
doorstep of the house in Adelphi Terrace where Barrie occupied the
top flat, even Alfred Butt had to exclaim, 'My dear, you look
absolutely ravishing'. Dressed in a turquoise silk dress by Poiret,
a chinchilla coat – to show she did not really need another one
– and a king's ransom in pearls casually draped around her neck,
it was Barrie himself who felt he was entertaining royalty. As,
indeed, with Gaby the unchallenged Queen of the Music Hall, he
was.

Over lunch, perhaps guessing at the superfluity of another
chinchilla coat, he said he would write a sketch for her instead.
Gaby was delighted. Later, as they left, the portly Alfred Butt

Gaby by John Kettlewell, 1913

following bemused and perplexed behind her, she ran down the stairs like a naughty little girl, giggling as she rang the doorbells of all the other apartments.

Barrie, then in his fifties, was at the very pinnacle of his fame. His career as writer and playwright had given the world such masterpieces as *The Admirable Crichton* and, of course, *Peter Pan*, and had made him a wealthy man in the process. He had latterly become fascinated by the music hall, and the possibilities it held for his own work. Entranced by Gaby's ethereal stage presence, and no doubt intrigued by the aura of scandal that surrounded her, he felt sure he could construct the perfect vehicle for her talents.

He wrote the sketch as promised, and it was anonymously incorporated into the programme at the Palace. To quote Barrie's biographer, Denis Mackail, the sketch was:

> '. . . something, so far as is remembered now, about a man offering her love instead of wealth – with special and subtle implications, of course, in this particular case. It got its laughs, and stayed on the bill; but Barrie, rehearsing again, and revelling in this new and surprising conjunction of personalities – for what other leading playwright or member of the Academic Committee could possibly find himself working and playing with Mlle Deslys? – became determined to provide her with a full-length revue.
>
> 'He told her – no doubt with some more magic here – and she at once fell in with the plan. One can't read her mind; one can only guess, and pretty hopelessly, at what she thought a revue by Barrie would be like. But all contracts and arrangements must be cleared out of the way so that she, Gaby Deslys, might be the latest Barrie star . . .'

Gaby could hardly believe this was happening. The friendship between the eminent baronet and the blonde *danseuse* became a subject for discussion over society dining tables all over London. No one could puzzle it out, it was such an unlikely alliance. Once again, the real details of the friendship go unrecorded; one can only guess as to its nature. They certainly spent a great deal of time together; many a lunchtime the electric brougham with its distinctive cane bodywork was spotted in Adelphi Terrace, the chauffeur, often liveried in colours that matched his mistress' latest outfits, passing the time walking the Old English sheepdog up and down the street.

This wholly unexpected and delightful turn of events made Gaby reluctant to leave London. But she had to. The Shuberts wanted her back in New York to finish her contract, despite the bad feelings that had existed between the brothers and their star at the end of her last trip. Gaby felt particularly worried about this, her third United States tour. She would rather have stayed in Europe. She made no bones about the fact that money was her only reason for going. She had no ties there, and few friends.

She had more than one reason for feeling nervous. Following the protests of early conservationists about the many species of rare birds being slaughtered for the feathers so highly prized by ladies of fashion, legislation had recently been introduced in America banning their importation. '"You can't have everything," as the customs officers will say as they amputate Gaby's aigrettes', one columnist gleefully predicted.

More serious was the problem that had been encountered by Marie Lloyd on entering the United States for her most recent tour. This best-loved of English music-hall artistes had been detained on the notoriously squalid Ellis Island by the immigration authorities, on the grounds that she was living with a man who was not her husband. A deportation order was issued together with one for Bernard Dillon, the well-known jockey with whom she had arrived. There was an enormous outcry in Britain. Quite apart from the hypocrisy of it – was America not supposed to be the Land of the Free? – this, they felt, was no way to treat a popular folk heroine.

Marie was later released, and said in an interview: 'I shall never appear again before the American public . . . I have withdrawn my appeal against the verdict of the immigration authorities, for I do not wish to remain a single day longer than necessary in a country which has treated me this way'. She later changed her mind and stayed on to fulfil her contracts.

Gaby was afraid lest an immigration authority which could refuse entry on the grounds of suggested immorality took a dim view of somebody the Church in England had deemed 'grossly indecent'. But she decided to take her chances. She said as much to the crowd of reporters seeing her off on the *Mauritania*, and added, 'Tell your Bishops I love them, but they show a little too much leg'.

10

THE FREAK SHOW

As Gaby was crossing the Atlantic in a very apprehensive state, the current revue at the Alhambra, *Keep Smiling*, had a scene set on the deck of a great liner. It went as follows:

> The purser says: 'Any passengers having valuables to entrust to my care, please step forward.'
> A maid struggles on with a huge hatbox as tall as herself, emblazoned with the name Maison Lewis. She is also carrying a tiny parcel.
> The purser asks what the hatbox is.
> The maid replies: 'A hat for Gaby Deslys.'
> 'And what is the small one, then?'
> 'Oh, this is her dress.'

It was a slight exaggeration, of course. Not in the enormity of the hat, but certainly in the brevity of her dress, and illustrative of the extent to which the whole scandal with the bishops had furthered Gaby's reputation as a wanton. If the Bishop of Kensington had been working as Gaby's press agent, he could hardly have made a better job of it. She had had a naughty reputation before, but she had a much racier one now.

She need not have worried about the immigration authorities, or the customs. She and Harry were not travelling as man and wife, and she could hardly be dumped on Ellis Island because of allegedly indecent performances in London. As for the feathers, $20,000-worth of bird of paradise and other assorted *aigrettes*, she managed to secure a temporary importation permit, leaving a bond that the offending objects would return to Europe when she did.

She had sailed easily through customs, but it wasn't long before other problems beset her. Her marmosets had proved too troublesome and demanding as pets, and their place in Gaby's affections had been taken by two tiny, hairless, Mexican chihuahuas.★ She had booked to stay at the Astor Hotel, but they used their 'no dogs' rule as an excuse not to admit her. After a loud exchange with the manager, Gaby decamped with her entourage to the Claridge, where she settled down to work out with the Shubert Brothers the details of the extensive tour they had planned for her before her contract with them finally ran out, in the spring of 1914. They were determined to get as much work out of her as possible. So far, she had only been seen in the eastern states. They planned to open her show in Pittsburgh, and from there go right the way through the mid-West, ending up in California at about Christmas time. Her new vehicle, *The Little Parisienne*, which opened at the Alvin in Pittsburgh on 24 November, also featured a performer who had herself been at the centre of a sensational scandal a few years earlier.

Evelyn Nesbit had married into the Thaw family, one of Pittsburgh's great dynasties, early in the century. Married bliss, such as it may have been, with a man whose drunkenness, addiction to cocaine and bizarre sexual practices would later become well-known, came abruptly to an end when her husband shot dead the famous architect Stanford White. Harry K. Thaw did this in full view of the audience at the Madison Square Garden theatre on 25 June 1906, on the opening night of a show called *Mamzelle Champagne*. He was subsequently committed to an insane asylum. His beautiful young bride was disowned by her society mother-in-law, and she was forced to earn her living as a vaudeville turn.† Needless to say, she was a far greater success as the notorious

---

★ Small dogs had become increasingly fashionable since the Pekinese had been imported into Europe in the nineteenth century. By 1910, *Punch* noted, 'The cult of the toy dog has reached a stage where ladies have to look at the little darlings through a microscope.'

† In 1917 Evelyn Nesbit cashed in on her disastrous marriage and made a semi-autobiographical film with her son, Russell Thaw, called *Redemption*. In later years, writing her memoirs became her only means of income. They were published in many forms, one of which was filmed in the 1950s as *The Girl in the Red Velvet Swing*, and in which the young Joan Collins played the starring rôle.

Evelyn Nesbit-Thaw than she had ever been as plain Evelyn Nesbit.

The fact that the Shubert Brothers had Gaby on the same bill as a woman whose only claim to fame was having married a murderer, was indicative of the way they were handling her. It was one of the reasons she was unhappy with their management, and eager for her contract to expire. But before this happened, she had a long and gruelling tour ahead of her.

The tour took her, amongst other places, to Kansas City, St Louis, Salt Lake City and, finally, San Francisco and Los Angeles. The normal ballyhoo surrounded her all the way. Her appearances in Salt Lake City engendered much publicity, and stories were printed that she had received an offer of marriage from a wealthy Mormon businessman who already had two wives. The idea did not appeal to Gaby any more than the thirty or so other offers of marriage that one newspaper reported she received on this trip. She was shocked by the casualness with which so many Americans treated this, for her, most serious of vows,* and by the alacrity with which so many wealthy men seemed willing to enter into marriage with someone they had never even met. She thought of these proposals as a joke in the worst possible taste; they were part of the sense of unreality that haunted Gaby throughout this American visit. The $6,000 per week she was being paid was the only reason she carried on, and at times even this did not seem compensation enough for all that she had to go through to earn it.

Variety claimed to be surprised that the Shuberts could pay her so much for her 'exhibition of lingerie' and still make a profit; but they apparently could, even in the face of stiff competition. Early in February, Gaby did a short season in Chicago with Gertrude Hoffman, Harry Lauder and Eva Tanguay playing simultaneously in neighbouring theatres.

Eva Tanguay was competition indeed. A big sexy redhead with a larger-than-life personality, she was one of the greatest figures on

* When Harry Fox divorced his wife to marry Jenny Dolly, whom he had met when they had both been appearing with Gaby in *Vera Violetta*, he was asked by the Divorce Court judge if he would like to pay his wife $25 per week maintenance. He replied, 'With much pleasure.' On leaving the court, he told reporters, 'I like the way they do business here, I'm always coming here for my divorces in future'.

the American vaudeville stage. She had a loud, unmusical voice, with which she used to belt out such numbers as, 'Go As Far As You Like', 'It's All Been Done Before, But Not The Way I Do It' and 'I Want Someone To Go Wild With Me', in such a calculatedly provocative way that she had many times crossed swords with the censors. If anyone was close to realizing the value of publicity as much as Gaby Deslys, it was Eva Tanguay. Unlike Gaby, she was even willing to pay for it herself, taking out full-page advertise-ments in *Variety* proclaiming her greatness. This expenditure made her a great favourite with that paper, which was as flattering to her as it was unkind to Gaby. This was particularly unfair because Tanguay herself admitted that her success was due to sensational publicity rather than to real talent. A little older than Gaby, she was of French and French-Canadian stock, and for the past decade and more had been terrorising her audiences with riotous displays of overt sexuality. A comedienne who sang and danced after a fashion, she had been called 'an electrified hoyden' and 'a one-woman wave of destruction'. Peter Leslie, in his detailed study of the music hall, *A Hard Act to Follow*, says of her:

'Offstage, Eva Tanguay was just impossible. She missed matinees if she felt tired, she assaulted chorines if she thought they were making eyes at her man; she would bawl out an audience, calling them small-town hicks if her dressing rooms weren't comfortable enough. Once she threw a stagehand downstairs because he got in her way when she was taking a curtain call. On one circuit the manager extracted a $5,000 cash bond from her to keep the peace and the terms of her engagement.'

One can be sure that Gaby stayed well out of her way. Especially as it was known that Tanguay resented the fact that the seats for Gaby's show were twice the price of hers, and that she was making much more money. This was, however, America's second-biggest city, so there was no shortage of theatregoers, and both theatres played to full houses, the Lauder and Hoffman shows also doing good business.

The Shuberts wanted to stage one final Broadway show featur-ing Gaby before her contract was up, and they had decided on a re-working of an old musical comedy called *The Girls from Kays*, re-titled *The Belle of Bond Street*. After much wrangling, with Gaby refusing to do it unless they could find a place in it for Harry, rehearsals started back in New York. Gaby was to appear with the veteran character actor Sam Bernard, as well as a beautiful young showgirl called Marion Davies – one day to become famous as the mistress of William Randolph Hearst. As usual, the Shuberts planned to open the show at the Hyperion, New Haven. When Gaby heard this, the awful memories of that night a couple of years earlier came flooding back. But she dismissed it from her mind. After all, lightning never strikes twice . . .

How wrong she was. The Yale students once again caused havoc. Marion Davies recalled: 'The Yalies took a dislike to the play and brought to a post-première performance rotten tomatoes, eggs, and other decaying matter. They threw it on the stage while Gaby Deslys was up front, and she took the brunt of it. She ran offstage weeping, with tomato running down her face.' Badly shaken but philosophical about it, Gaby at least had the pleasure of seeing the major troublemakers in the audience arrested, thrown in jail, and fined. On Broadway, the show got a better reception, and the reviews were generally enthusiastic.

Whilst Gaby appeared in Chicago, one of the neighbouring theatres featured an act in which Gertrude Hoffman performed a particularly unflattering impression of Gaby and her partner 'Harry Pilsner'. Gaby had found this sufficiently offensive to take out a successful court injunction to stop her doing it. Litigation of one sort or another had become a part of Gaby's everyday life. She had fallen in with the American way of settling any kind of dispute with professional parties or private individuals – suing them. As well as initiating such actions, she found herself at the receiving end of many, having processes served on her for real and imagined breaches of contract. Soon she took it all for granted. She employed the services of several top American lawyers, particularly one she had met in San Diego, Charlie Hanlon. They had become good friends. Gaby was intrigued by this man, who had built his own impressive tomb, complete except for the space left on the tombstone where the date of his death would be added.

In Europe, Gaby usually found that tradespeople of all types were happy to give her hefty discounts on their products, in return for the resultant publicity. This system did not work in America, and she often felt, quite correctly, that public knowledge of her huge salary resulted in prices being doubled whenever she was known to be the customer. This really annoyed her, and she frequently refused to pay bills she considered inflated. Once again, she would find herself being sued, often under dramatic circumstances.

One night in New York early in May 1914, as the curtain came down on *The Belle of Bond Street*, a young man made his way to the stage and followed Gaby to her dressing room. As she closed her door, he called her by name, throwing an envelope at her. Gaby, alarmed by the intruder, screamed. Some of the chorus girls also screamed, and the young man fled out of the stage door and along Forty-fourth Street, pursued by a couple of hefty stagehands. Someone shouted 'Stop, thief!' and several theatregoers joined in the chase. At Broadway the fugitive ran into the arms of a policeman, just as the first stagehand overtook him. He was taken back to the theatre, where the missile he had thrown at Gaby was recovered. It was a summons, and the 'thief' was only a lawyer's clerk doing his job of serving it.

On this occasion, she was being sued by a Boston lawyer called Sullivan. He had asked Gaby for $1,400 for some legal work he had done. She was horrified at the size of this sum, and intended to make him wait for his money. Although she eventually settled with him to the tune of $500, she did not do so until the day before she left the country. There were also several smaller claims pending against her. In addition to these irritations, her relationship with the Shuberts had not improved; she was barely speaking to them. *Variety* continued to lambast her on an almost weekly basis,* and all in all she felt that this trip had been a disaster in every way, apart from the money. She was longing to get home.

But before she left, the most important matter she had to settle was that of her film debut, which she was particularly eager to make – if the price was right.

In the few years since the first movies had been made, film

---

* *Variety* christened her, along with Charlie Chaplin and Harry Lauder, one of the three 'greatest savers' in the business.

production had increased by leaps and bounds, and all the major stage stars had signed up with the numerous production companies that were being formed. These contracts were mostly single-picture deals, and Gaby had received many offers, none of which she found interesting. Hal Reid had recently offered her $9,000, but she did not think it sufficient. She knew what she was talking about. Sam Bernard, her co-star in *Belle of Bond Street*, had arranged to film *A Dangerous Maid* for $10,000, and she was a bigger draw than he was. Adolf Zukor's company, 'Famous Players', were also courting her, but as a Zukor spokesman told *Variety*, 'She wanted all kinds of money', and the filming completed in the five days between *Belle of Bond Street* finishing and her sailing back to Europe. Gaby invariably got her way with theatre managements, including the fees she demanded. They had made big profits out of her, so if she was going to have a movie career, she would run it along the same lines, or not at all.

She sailed out of New York on the *Imperator* on 22 May 1914. Her travelling companions were Harry Pilcer and the famous American comedienne Norah Bayes. This time there was no black maid to fall overboard, no baby crocodile either. She just took with her the $100,000 she had saved on the trip, and a movie contract signed by Adolf Zukor for one film, which guaranteed her $15,000 plus five per cent of the gross box-office profit. She also got $3,000 in advance, and a clause giving her total freedom of choice of material.

As usual, Gaby had got her own way.

11
A HUNDRED POUNDS
A NIGHT

The applause was thunderous as Gaby came forward to take her bow. Only one member of the audience was not applauding. Smiling bitterly, the good-looking woman in the stage box reached into her handbag and produced a small pistol. Taking careful aim, she pointed it at the small, curtseying figure at the footlights. The noise of the report was barely heard above the tumult created by the crowd, but as individual members of the audience realized what had happened, the cheers turned to gasps of horror. After a few seconds of stunned silence, someone screamed.

It was a perfect take. The movie, Gaby's first, was called *Her Triumph*, and it was being shot in Paris by Adolph Zukor's 'Famous Players' film company during the summer of 1914. Gaby had taken a big hand in writing the screenplay of this 'novel comedy-drama of the stage'. Much of the action was set backstage in a theatre, so she felt quite at home. The plot was a simple one, and despite the fact that it contained many elements that have since become cinematic clichés, it was very effective. The story opens with Gaby, a humble chorus girl with ambition, who supports her blind sister and invalid mother. At the theatre, she rivals the leading lady in the affections of her leading man. The star, in a fit of rage, threatens to walk out unless Gaby is dismissed. Her scheme fails, and Gaby ends up playing the starring role. The ex-leading lady tries to get revenge in several ways apart from shooting at – and missing – our heroine, including having her kidnapped by a band of villainous *apaches*.

A three-reeler, *Her Triumph* was shot in just a few days, Gaby taking to the new medium effortlessly. She looked beautiful on film and was fortunate in being so photogenic. Some well-known stage stars were not, and they consequently failed to make a successful transition from theatre to film. For example, 'Doris Keene fails to screen', the *Evening News* announced in 1920.

Gaby applied the same professionalism to her movie-making as she did to all her work, and the shooting went off without a hitch. She was very pleased with the results, realizing the importance of the new medium in bringing her performance to an ever-larger audience. Quite apart from the huge salaries successful movie stars could make, the general financial benefits of such universal advertising were inestimable. Gaby had no delusions about the fact that she had been made by publicity, but ever since the Manuel affair she never had to seek it; journalists followed her everywhere. In the interviews she readily gave to them, she pandered more and more to the popular myths that had grown up around her, and told the public what she thought it wanted to hear. And that did not always mean the truth.

For example, returning home on the *Imperator* from her last American trip, she was interviewed by a lady reporter working for the London weekly, *Tit-Bits*. In it, she 'divulged' some of her 'beauty secrets', claiming that her looks and figure were not achieved merely by diet and exercise, but that she required the daily ministrations of a manicurist, a hairdresser, a masseuse, and a make-up artist. Anyone who knew her well realized that this was nonsense. Apart from the occasional massage and haircut, she fulfilled all of these duties herself, once confiding in her dresser that she washed her own hair every day using 'a penny packet of Lux'. Whilst she made sure that the lady's maids she hired were adept at hairdressing, she always did her own make-up. When she made any appearances in public, as she often did at the races and other social occasions, or merely walking in the Bois de Boulogne, it was hard to believe that she had achieved the whole startling effect almost unassisted.

The summer of 1914 was, paradoxically, both peaceful and filled with incident. Gaby, very much enjoying being back in Paris, led a life that was as leisurely as it could be for anyone with so much energy. During the morning, she worked hard at Stillson's dance studio in the company of other music-hall stars, including Spinelly, who said of the studio, 'It's a place where there ain't no ten commandments, and the cushions are never straight'. She spent the remaining part of her days making plans for forthcoming appearances, being fitted for dresses, and controlling her ventures, the newest of which was the purchase of a block of flats at 37, rue Cortambert, a beautiful, newly finished building in the chic sixteenth *arrondissement* of Paris. She had bought it with the money she had earned in America. So, in the end, it had been worth enduring the hard work, the gruelling tours, the arguing, the law suits, the insults.

She felt that a new phase of her life was beginning; she began to feel that she had achieved her long-cherished ambition for security; that she would no longer be haunted by the spectre of the aged actress who had died in poverty. Although she had always been very selective about both the content of her act, and where she was prepared to perform, money had always been her prime motivating factor. Now she felt sufficiently comfortable to pursue projects that might satisfy another craving that she had, to her surprise, begun to develop – one for respectability.

The publicity surrounding *A la Carte*, although enormously profitable financially, had left an unpleasant after-taste. Gaby felt that her image had been cheapened. Despite what anyone might have thought, and the frivolous image of her purveyed by the world's press, she had always seen herself as a serious artist, instead of which she had been painted as a scarlet woman, her name synonymous with every kind of loose living. To some extent she was to blame for her immoral public image. The public knew very little of her private life because she was never willing to divulge details of it in press interviews. Consequently, the public identified her with the women she portrayed on stage: carefree *demimondaines*, eager to strip off and cavort with a variety of lovers. The statement she had made in reply to the *New York Journal* article about her in 1911 had done little to dispel the myth of her immorality. When she had said 'My time is money', many people had taken her literally. She had been shocked and hurt when rumours current at the time of *A la Carte* reached her ears.

The scandalmongers claimed she was the world's most expensive whore, charging £25 for a lunch date, £50 for dinner, and £100 to spend the night.

This was all far from the truth. Prostitution, even at this level – and it is worth bearing in mind that in 1913 £100 was as much as some domestic servants earned in two years – was not her métier. When she had brief relationships with very wealthy men, they were of her choosing, and the choice was not solely dependent upon how much money they had. On her most recent trip to America, she had been questioned by reporters about a rumour that she was to marry Frank J. Gould, one of the wealthiest men in America. She had told them, 'When I marry, it will be for love. I am not short of money'.

It is remarkable how persistent stories about her so-called 'immorality' have remained, and are still repeated by theatrical old-timers who never knew Gaby personally.

Ironically enough, this early sex symbol led a comparatively chaste existence, especially following her meeting with Harry. She had never met anyone that she really cared about as much, and she wanted to marry him even though he was penniless. One of the reasons she had always been so ambitious was that she valued her independence above all else. That independence, and the career that gave it to her, was her *raison d'être*. If money had been the most important thing in her life, she could have married an old multi-millionaire years before. She had certainly had enough offers.

By 1914 Gaby was resigned to the fact that Harry was not going to provide her with the stable emotional relationship that she longed for, primarily because of his sexual ambiguity. He was, nevertheless, the closest friend she had ever had, and despite its increasingly turbulent nature, their friendship continued. Harry was as strong-willed and independently minded as she was, and after three years of being constantly in Gaby's company, he was itching to try his luck alone. He had been unknown when they met, but he was convinced that he would have been successful without her help; that Gaby had merely been the catalyst in his inevitable rise to fame. Their rows became more frequent and bitter, but the bond between them persisted. Theirs seemed to be a relationship that thrived on friction.

They were drawn closer by a dramatic incident that occurred on 14 July 1914. On this day, accompanied by other members of the acting profession, they attended a dinner party hosted by the celebrated actor and comedian Max Linder, at his luxurious riverside home at Varennes, outside Paris. After dinner, the party went down to watch a Bastille Day fireworks display taking place on the opposite bank of the river. Suddenly, the old landing stage on which they were standing collapsed, dropping the whole party into the river. Gaby, normally a strong swimmer, was pulled down into the current by the voluminous beaded cape she was wearing, and would certainly have drowned, had Harry not dragged her ashore. Frightened and shaken by the incident, she developed a chill, and had to spend a week or so in bed before travelling with Harry to London to make arrangements for her autumn appearance at the Palace. Once there, she claimed to have recovered fully, but contemporary photographs show her looking pale and unwell.

In London, she arranged with Alfred Butt that she would replace a beautiful young American actress, Elsie Janis, as the main attraction in the hit revue of the year, *The Passing Show*. Whilst there, she renewed her friendship with Sir James Barrie, and he excitedly revealed to her details of his projected revue for 1915, in which she was to star. Other literary giants were busy exploring the music-hall medium, but not always with success. That very year, even George Bernard Shaw had toyed with it, but his sketch, *The Music Cure*, produced at the Palace in April, had been a resounding flop. It was as well that his new play at His Majesty's – *Pygmalion*, with Sir Herbert Tree and Mrs Patrick Campbell – had received great critical acclaim.

Gaby returned to Paris to organize the costumes for *The Passing Show*, feeling that the future looked bright indeed. But it was not to be. By the first days of August, Germany had invaded Belgium, and there was already fighting in north-eastern France. On 4 August war was declared. Gaby, who was in Ostend for the weekend, sailed immediately to England. Everyone had been taken by surprise, and there was a period of stunned inactivity before the full weight of what had happened hit home. But before long, recruiting began in earnest; young men of every class volunteered their services and sailed off to the muddy battlefields of France and Belgium.

12

THE RIGHT
CONNECTIONS

Gaby's opening at the Palace had to be delayed, for her costumes, made by Callot, were still in Paris. They eventually arrived in time for her to make her appearance on 21 September in a piece entitled *The Rajah's Ruby*. A concentrated drama in five acts, written by Arthur Wimperis and Hartley Carrick, this was 'a pretty witless affair', according to *Tatler*, but nevertheless a great personal triumph for her. The applause began long before she appeared, and when the curtain fell she was called before it a dozen times and compelled to deliver a speech. From this night on, her whole public image was to change. As a world-famous Frenchwoman, she would become a symbol of the Alliance, as famous for her war work as she had been for her pearls.

Meanwhile, she and Harry were getting along no better, their arguments and disagreements backstage at the Palace taking place almost nightly. One cause of dissent was Harry's jealousy about Gaby's salary. A typical row is related in the memoirs of Alastair Mackintosh, a friend of Basil Hallam, who was their co-star in *The Rajah's Ruby*.

'In her dressing room one night, Harry came in while I was talking to her. He was very excitable, having apparently just discovered her earnings, which in those days were the highest paid to any artist save an operatic star.

' "It's not fair", he protested, pacing up and down. "It's just not fair that you should be getting five hundred and fifty pounds a week and I only fifty. You ought to give me some of it, Gaby. After all, I made you."

'She swung round from her dressing table and, hurling a scalding French epithet at him, added furiously, "You didn't make me! The King of Portugal made me!"'

Basil Hallam did his best to calm them both down, but to no avail. Hallam, the archetypal *knut*, as the suave and witty playboys of the period preceding the war were called, was hopelessly in love with Gaby, though few people knew this, least of all Gaby herself. The most tragic aspect of his passion was that it would be his last before he died the following year, an early victim of the war.

Having reconciled herself to the fact that her friendship with Harry was, despite its intensity, going to remain just a friendship, Gaby felt free to involve herself in another relationship. For some months, she had been avidly pursued by one of London's most colourful and popular figures, Gordon Selfridge. Being in his mid-fifties, he was a little old for her taste, but despite his years, he was still a magnetically attractive and dynamic man. He was also extremely generous with the vast profits he was making from his department store, which was at this time the most fashionable in London. He had a weakness for women who, like himself, were great achievers, and he had a particular penchant for famous dancers. Despite being married, his attachments to both Anna Pavlova and Isadora Duncan were well-known.

Harry Gordon Selfridge was born in Ripon, Wisconsin, in 1856. He had been abandoned when very young by a father who had gone off to fight in the Civil War, and who had never returned. Consequently, he was brought up by his strong-willed mother, who had great ambitions for her son, and she remained a life-long influence on and inspiration to him.

He had started his working life at the age of fourteen as a bank clerk, earning $20 a week. He possessed a natural gift for commerce, and this, combined with considerable flair and imagination, eventually won him the post of general retail manager of the largest store in Chicago, Marshall Fields, where his tremendous drive earned him the nickname 'Mile-a-minute-Harry'. He was made a junior partner in the business in 1890, and under his management Marshall Fields became one of the leading stores in the United States. He introduced such innovations as lifts, revolving front doors, and window displays that remained illuminated at night. Visits to Europe had given him a taste for culture and luxury, and when in 1890 he married the beautiful socialite Rosalie Amelia Buckingham, his wedding gift to his bride was a necklace of blue diamonds.

On failing to be offered a senior partnership, he left Marshall Fields in 1904 to set up his own store in competition, but after a short time he sold this business, at a huge profit. For many years he had dreamed of having his own shop in London, where he felt certain a fortune could be reaped using his formidable marketing expertise. His dream was finally realized when the department store that still bears his name was opened in 1909, at a cost of £400,000. Profits in the first few years grew larger and larger, due, amongst other things, to brilliant publicity gimmicks that Selfridge thought up, including having on display in the store the aircraft in which Blériot made his historic Channel crossing. He was a born showman, and extravagantly generous. Eventually, he dissipated his entire fortune. A lover of luxury and high style, and a great connoisseur of feminine beauty, he had become besotted with Gaby, and was eager to indulge her tastes, to lavish on her a fortune in jewels, furs and *objets d'art*.

Meanwhile, she and Harry had decided that they would try to work apart. When *The Rajah's Ruby* closed early in the New Year, Gaby would immediately begin rehearsals for the Barrie revue, and Harry would partner a girlfriend of his from New York called Teddie Gerrard, at the London Pavilion. They came to this agreement with the minimum of bad feeling, both eager for a change.

The Rajah's Ruby was a comparative success, considering that there was a war on but, with vastly depleted audiences, the theatre in general was set for a decline.

One morning, just before Christmas, Gaby awoke feeling terrible. She had not felt very strong in the months since her unexpected dip in the Seine, but she had taken little time off. Consequently, there were days when she felt a little off-colour, but this morning it was more than just that. As the day wore on, her throat felt increasingly sore, and by the afternoon she realized that something was seriously wrong. She summoned her doctor, and he

105

immediately rushed her to hospital for an emergency operation on her vocal chords. It was another manifestation of the inexplicable inherent throat weakness that had dogged her all her life, and which would, intermittently, continue to do so.

She had been scheduled to finish at the Palace a week or so later, but Alfred Butt came to visit her the day after the operation and told her that Ethel Levey had stepped in to replace her, and not to worry about a thing. Christmas Day found her lying in bed, still muzzy from the anaesthetic, surrounded by flowers. A basket of white lilies from Gordon Selfridge reached almost to the ceiling. As usually happened when she was ill, she yearned to be back home in the South of France. She determined to return for a while as soon as she was well enough to travel, war or no war.

The Allied success at the Battle of the Marne had checked German advances into France, so it seemed that she would be able to make the trip in relative safety. It would also be a good opportunity for her to see that her properties in Paris had come to no harm, and to be reunited with her mother, who had travelled back to the south at the outbreak of the war. Perhaps, she thought, she would also visit her father. Although he had never approved of her lifestyle, her attitude towards him had mellowed. He was an old man now, and she had heard that his health was failing. It made her sad to feel that he might die before they could reconcile their differences. Although she had no intention of returning as the repentant prodigal daughter, she considered acting the part out for the old man's peace of mind.

By the New Year Gaby had gone, leaving Harry preparing for his debut with a new partner, and Sir James Barrie anxiously awaiting the return of his newest star. She arrived back early in February of 1915, refreshed by her convalescence and eager to get back into harness. Her father had been extremely weak, but as stubborn as ever. She had watched his coolness towards her melt a little; had even detected a little pride in the fact that his daughter had become so famous. She had taken pains to assure him that not everything he read in the papers was true. 'They will print anything to get a good story', she had told him. 'I never bother denying the lies. After all, it keeps the public interested in me.' He had seemed reassured, and they had parted amicably.

106

In London, she moved into a new house next-door to the Albert Hall, at number 13, Kensington Gore. It was on a long lease, which was purportedly bought by Gordon Selfridge for £4,000. He was still married, and therefore his affair with Gaby had to be handled discreetly. However, it was not handled discreetly enough. Several of the Selfridges staff knew that on Sunday afternoon their boss was in the habit of taking Gaby through the shop, where she was given anything that took her fancy. She had always appreciated a bargain, but this was almost too good to be true. She must have spent long hours in the jewellery department. Superstitious as ever, the first thing she did on moving in to the Georgian terraced town house with its leaded windows and view across Hyde Park, was to change the number to 12A. And, with her weekly shopping excursions to Selfridges, it was decorated and furnished in no time.

Gaby's friendship with Barrie prospered, to the continued amazement of society – 'The astonishing fact of the matter is that it's a *personal* friendship', wrote the *Tatler* – and his generosity towards her was unabated. In fact, her affair with Gordon Selfridge seemed to spur Barrie on to new heights of magnanimity. He never gave her a chinchilla coat, but there were other gifts in abundance. As far as she was concerned, the greatest gift he could bestow on her was respectability, which he did merely by associating with her.

She threw herself into rehearsals with a vengeance. Barrie wrote in one of his many letters to his friend Guy du Maurier, 'I have never known man or woman on the stage with such a capacity for work, and always so gracious to everybody, that they are all at her feet . . .' He was disarmed by, amongst other things, her candour, and after many years of dealing with the inflated egos and pretensions of so many actresses, he was refreshed by a personality so undeluded as to be able to state, as she did one day in rehearsal, 'I can't sing, I can't dance, but I can do it!'

Barrie was further enchanted by the child-woman aspect of her personality. Denis Mackail, in his official biography of Barrie, *The Story of JMB*, says: 'Here was, or should have been, the fulfilment of not only his promises of eighteeen months ago, but of a much older dream. To have the fluffiest, fairest and most feminine of all actresses, and one who stood for these qualities all over the world, awaiting his command.' Her equivocally girlish, fairy-like stage presence so tinged with overt sexuality thrilled him; but as rehearsals went on, it became increasingly clear that he was unsure of how to utilize it. As the revue, entitled *Rosy Rapture, or The Pride of the Beauty Chorus*, unfolded, this uncertainty became painfully obvious. Gaby did her best with the material but she did not seem to know what he wanted from her any more than he did. She desperately wanted the show to be a success, and tried especially hard to please Barrie, who was even at the best of times a difficult and increasingly withdrawn personality.

Nothing, however, that Gaby or anyone else could do would alleviate Barrie's profound grief at the death in action of his great friend Guy du Maurier, which was rapidly followed by that of his adopted son, George Llewelyn Davies. Barrie was so stricken that he could not bring himself to attend the final rehearsals of the revue, and on the opening night at the Duke of York's, on 22 March 1915, the author of the piece was conspicuous by his absence. This opening night was, as *The Era* said, 'an overpoweringly smart affair'. A glittering first-night audience included the Duchess of Rutland with her two beautiful daughters, Lady Anglesey and Lady Diana Manners, as well as Lady Gwendoline Churchill, the Hon. Mrs Trefusis, and many other members of the *beau monde*; theatrical and literary personalities such as Ethel Levey, Pauline Chase, Cissie Loftus and Arnold Bennett and, of course, Harry Pilcer.

The area surrounding the theatre was completely jammed with traffic, and the house was crammed to capacity. There had been a tremendous build-up in the press; the unlikely alliance of Gaby and Barrie made 'the Gabarrie Revue' the most eagerly awaited theatrical event of the year, and, according to the *Tatler*, it was considered 'the height of bad form not to adore Gaby'. The curtain went up on the first act, a short one-act play typical of Barrie's style entitled *The New Word*, about an ordinary family involved in the war. Superbly written and acted though it was, it hardly consti-tuted an appropriate opener for a light-hearted revue. Soldiers on leave from the appalling conditions at The Front did not need reminding of the war. The audience was, therefore, in a rather sombre frame of mind for the main body of the programme and, although it had its witty moments, as when the heroine was crushed by the 'superbly incompetent chorus' every time she tried to sing, and Gaby supplied all her usual glamour, by the end of the evening it was clear that many things needed changing.

Gaby received her ovation amidst dozens of enormous baskets of flowers, some seven or eight feet high, and mostly sent by Gordon Selfridge. She bowed and blew kisses to an audience largely eager to escape from an evening that had gone on far too long. The elements of success had certainly been there: the music had been written by John Crook of *Peter Pan* fame, as well as by Herman Darewski; and there were a couple of numbers by the then comparatively unknown Jerome Kern. Barrie had also used some cinematography, which was quite an innovation when included in a review in this way, although a film show to finish the evening's entertainment had become quite common in the music hall. But, in the final analysis, the production by Dion Boucicault was too serious and heavy. It did not have 'nearly enough champagne . . . to carry the thing along,' wrote Mackail in his *Story of JMB*. And, as for Gaby, she had done her best, but to little avail. Next day, *The Times* said:

'Apparently Miss Gaby Deslys is an institution, she must be nothing less than that to have a revue written on purpose for her by Sir James Barrie. And as soon as you set eyes on her you know it; you can see it in her gait, in her daring costumes and her daring semi-nudes, in the way she takes the stage, in her whole behaviour.

'Obviously, irresistibly, triumphantly, she is an institution.

'Also, by fits and starts, she is an artist. Literally by fits and starts, for it is when she dances. She can dance you any dance – the dance graceful and *legato*, the dance comic and staccato, the dance epileptic and frenzied. It is here that she is really rapturous, with the joy of the artist in creating art. Further, she is an everlasting high-pressure source of energy, never at rest and, as people say, all over the place.

'Your resultant impression of her is, perhaps, rather mixed. You are fascinated by her dancing, repelled by something "macabre" about her, enlivened, and in the end rather fatigued, by her enormous energy. We speak for what Shakespeare called "the general". No doubt for special tastes Miss Deslys

109

offers special provocations. The devotees of dress must worship her. Amateurs of bare backs must find her priceless. English people who like to have their language tortured out of recognition must revel in her. But in the end you have to come back to the old view; she is an institution, something not to be missed, a theme for dinner-table and smoking-room gossip. And now her talent has been hallmarked "J.M.B." in the corner!

'We wish we could recognise the process as reciprocal; we wish "G.D." in the corner could hallmark Sir James' talent. To be frank, it does not. If it were not for the name on the playbill and some mechanical jokes on the stage, we would never have detected Sir James' hand in this revue . . . but it all comes back in the end to the institution, to Miss Deslys and her wonderful dances, and her wonderful dresses, and her rather sick smile, and her incomprehensible jargon, and her celebrated expanse of bare back. If you are more attracted than repelled by her you will be more pleased than bored by *Rosy Rapture*.'

Although unusually unkind to Gaby personally, this was the general tone of the reviews published at the time. But Barrie was not going to yield without a struggle to public opinion that the revue had failed. Denis Mackail says: 'He was back in the theatre at once for more rehearsals, and cuts, and alterations, and always with the feeling that something could still be saved if the right changes could be made. And the returns weren't exactly disastrous, though there were always empty seats.' Gaby's and, indeed, J.M.B.'s following ensured that the box office was kept alive, but, as though things were not already bad enough, the worst disaster was yet to come.

Barrie was convinced that Charles Frohman, with his enormous reserves of expertise and experience, would be able to pull the show together. Their long and successful collaboration had resulted in a string of successes, and Barrie's confidence in this old and dear friend was unshakeable. So he sent a wire to New York, begging him to come at once. On 1 May, Frohman boarded a liner for England, the name of which would become synonymous with disaster – the *Lusitania*. On 7 May, with the coast of Ireland in sight, two torpedoes were fired from a German submarine, and the giant liner sank almost at once. Of over 1,800 people on board, 1,200 were lost. Charles Frohman was among them. For *Rosy Rapture*, this was the death knell. In his grief, Barrie lost all interest in the show, and on 29 May the curtain came down for the last time.

Gaby had no choice but to adopt a stoical attitude towards the whole disastrous affair. Barrie in no way held her responsible for what was one of the biggest flops of his career, although most of Barrie's many biographers attribute the failure of *Rosy Rapture* to Gaby's 'lack of talent' rather than his inadequacy as a revue writer. Their friendship continued, and her gaiety and glamour undoubtedly brought a little light into his unhappy life. Her visits to Adelphi Terrace were frequent. Although the nature of this friendship has never been fully explained, it was almost certainly platonic, although Barrie may have got a vicarious pleasure from people thinking otherwise. Later in the year, he collaborated with Gaby in adapting excerpts from *Rosy Rapture* for her use on her tour of the provinces.

In the meantime, despite the failure of *Rosy Rapture*, she had much to be grateful for. She had become one of the most fashionable figures in London. The *Tatler* featured her in every issue of that year, and she was generally described in the most glowing terms. For example: '. . . by the way, the Gabs, you know, is really a very attractive little person, and not so spoiled as she might be, off the stage, I mean'.

On a personal level, she was as happy as she had ever been. She had managed to find time to supervise the decoration of her new house, and when it was finished, she was only too happy to let the press in to have a look. It was as extravagantly furnished as anyone would expect, featuring room after room decorated in what Cecil Beaton gleefully called, 'sumptuously bad taste'. There was a smoking room in the Turkish style, piled high with gold brocade cushions and lit with a mosque lamp that might have come out of the Alhambra's foyer, and a panelled dining room in the Old English style, complete with a massive refectory table, and enough antique pewter and brass to set up several shops in Portobello Road.

The bedroom was extraordinary, dominated by a vast carved and gilded four-poster bed which was raised up on a dais strewn with chinchilla rugs. On the wall at its head, between the back posts, a large crucifix shone, the small window behind making it seem to emit rays of divine light. The opposite end of the room contained a life-size Madonna, with votive candles permanently flickering before her. It was impossible to imagine anything of an indecent nature taking place in this room. Indeed, with its pious yet ostentatious atmosphere, it could have been the home of a nun who had renounced her vows and then won the football pools. It was certainly a setting more suitable for spiritual rather than carnal gratification. The physical side of her relationship with Gordon Selfridge could hardly have been indulged here.

Gaby had little time to spend lazily enjoying her new home, although she made room in her schedule to entertain Matichon on one of her sister's rare visits to London. After her departure, it was back to a routine consisting of at least eight shows a week, and many days doing her own brand of war work: collecting money for the French Relief Fund, entertaining parties of wounded soldiers to tea. She was even photographed riding a motorcycle down Knightsbridge, with a wounded officer as passenger in her sidecar.

Whenever there was a charity fête, Gaby was there. The youthful Cecil Beaton saw her on one such occasion, and she made a lasting impression. He noted her fine magenta lace dress, her hat trimmed with magenta osprey. '. . . Magenta orchids trembled at her breast; magenta were her lace stockings, and her shoes were of magenta satin with magenta ribbons criss-crossed up her legs. Pale magenta cheeks and lips had been painted on a face the colour of marshmallow. Vulgar? Perhaps, but by whose standards? The gesture seemed to transcend vulgarity and create its own allure.'*

At the Theatrical Garden Party that summer, Gaby saw an officer she knew coming towards her, and she threw out both her hands in welcome. Suddenly, she saw that he had no hands to give her, only stumps swathed in bandages. She cried out, shocked beyond words, and burst into tears. After that, she vowed to do all she possibly could to help the Allied cause, assisting in recruiting drives in London and, later in the year, all over the provinces. One night at the Camberwell Palace Music Hall, she made a promise of a kiss to every new recruit, and laughingly kept it as dozens of young men leapt out of the audience to sign up.

*From *The Glass of Fashion* by Cecil Beaton.

She wrote an article in the *Tatler* entitled 'Why We Are Wanted in Wartime', in which she stated that she had considered the possibility of becoming a Red Cross nurse. Of course, it was a ridiculous suggestion, and no one took her seriously, but her further statements on the role she saw for herself in the war – that of entertainer *par excellence*, helping soldiers on leave forget the horror of trench warfare – were genuinely moving. She was already the soldier's favourite pin-up. Cut-out portraits of her decorated the makeshift quarters of Allied troops at the Front. She was the Betty Grable of the trenches, and as such, she fulfilled a far more important role than she could ever have done as a nurse.

13
5064 GERRARD

One of the most successful revues of the war years opened at the Alhambra about the same time as *Rosy Rapture*. André Charlot, who had graduated from his position as the Alhambra's Paris representative to that of its manager, replacing Alfred Moul in 1912, had planned an evening's entertainment that would help people forget, at least for a couple of hours, the terrors of the war. In it there would be no patriotism or pageants; in fact, there would be no mention whatever of the one topic that monopolized the headlines and thoughts of the country. The purpose of this new revue would be to 'brighten and amuse', and to this end, Charlot planned a show that would rival anything the Gaiety or Daly's could offer in the way of pretty girls, lavish costumes and fast comedy. He advertised for pretty chorus girls, and, with the war bringing a slump in the demand for their services, 500 turned up for the sixteen available places.

Charlot did not like the revue's original title, *1915*, and decided to run a competition to find a suitable name for it. The sum of five guineas was offered to the winner, and over 8,000 people replied to advertisements placed in the popular press. The only stipulations were that the title should consist of no more than four words, and should make no reference or allusion to the war. The winner, *5064 Gerrard*, was the telephone number of the Alhambra. Skilful publicist that he was, Charlot then launched an attention-grabbing advertizing campaign, with the number cryptically plastered all over London – on the sides of buses, in the Underground and on hoardings everywhere. So successful was this campaign that, by the time the curtain went up on 15 March, advance bookings ensured full houses for months ahead.

In later years, Charlot's name would become associated with a whole succession of fast-moving, polished and witty revues. *5064*

GABY ENTHRONED
The Most Famous of the Gay Inhabitants of the Gay City.

Gaby 'enthroned' following the Manuel scandal, May 1911

Matichon, Paris 1911

À La Carte, 1913

Gaby and Harry, publicity shot, 1913

The costume that led to complaints from the Bishop of Kensington – her legs are visible under the harem pants, *À La Carte*, 1913

Gaby's bedroom at 12a Kensington Gore

Gaby in *Rosy Rapture*, 1915

On the steps of 12a Kensington Gore

5064 Gerrard

The feathers for this hat cost £200 in 1912

The symbol of the Alliance. Gaby in her allied flags costume made especially for America Day, April 20, 1917 and worn in *Suzette*

Fund raising from her car on **French Flag Day, 1915**

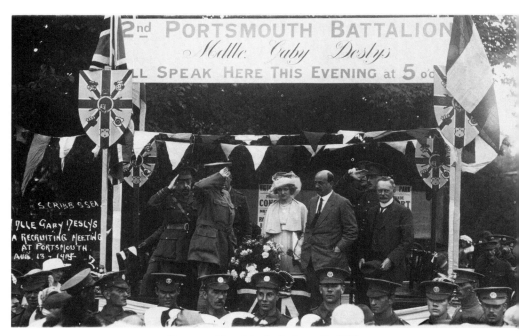

On a recruiting drive in Portsmouth, 1915

Gaby entertains Matichon at 12a Kensington Gore 1915. Note the orchid centrepiece

In Charles Burnel's gallery choosing the props for *Les débuts de Chichine*

Gaby as Little Emily in J. M. Barrie's *Rosy Rapture*

Gerrard was one of the first. The array of talent on show included Lee White; Phyllis Monkman and Robert Hale, one of the most gifted comedians ever to grace the variety stage; as well as a newcomer, Beatrice Lillie, in one of her first appearances on the London stage. Her number, entitled 'I want to go back to Michigan', required her to be dressed as a farm boy. This rather butch image suited her so well that it took her years to escape from it.

Robert Hale was totally at home in revue and had a fine understanding of it, as revealed in an interview he gave just before the opening of *5064 Gerrard*. He said: 'In revue an actor has to grip his audience right away. Heavy work is a mistake. No section of the house attends a revue to be made to think'. In *5064 Gerrard* he gripped his audience in many hysterical scenes, including one set in a courtroom, in which the principal characters were 'The Man', 'The Woman' and 'Their Terrible Trial', with Hale taking the last-named part as a very large little girl. A note on the programme regarding this scene stated that, 'The revolving stage patented by the Alhambra will support the weight of the entire company, including the celebrated child-actress'.

The turn that really brought the house down was a sketch in act two called 'At Murray's Club'. In this, Robert Hale was billed as 'Miss Rosy Rapture' and, suitably dressed in an extravagant hat and a frock with miles of lampshade fringing and festooned with pearls the size of golf balls, he danced with a certain 'revue author' clad in a short kilt and half-bald wig. Even without the outrageous 'gliding' choreography of the dance, and Robert Hale's lyrics for the song – 'Frenchie-Scottie' – there could be no doubt in anyone's mind who they were supposed to be. Hysterical laughter nightly rocked the Alhambra. Heaven knows what Gaby must have thought of this wickedly funny send-up of her, which was playing to packed houses just around the corner from where her own revue was dying on its feet. Yet, ever quick to see an opportunity for turning disaster to her advantage, when Charlot approached her with an offer to join the revue after *Rosy Rapture* closed, she was pleased to accept. She was astute enough to know that if the Alhambra was making money out of her – albeit by way of satire – she might as well get in on what was, after all, her own act. Bearing in mind how strained relations had been between Charlot and Gaby when he had been the Alhambra's Paris agent, how difficult and greedy he had considered her then, it would be interesting to know exactly how the terms were negotiated.

Charlot agreed to make a few changes to the script. At Gaby's insistence, the Barrie character was written out, and Harry Pilcer was written in. Harry's season with Teddie Gerrard had gone well enough, but he had not found her personality easy to deal with. She drank too much, and was given to displays of aggressive temper that made Gaby seem saintly by comparison. Gaby, too, had been less than happy with Jules Raucourt, her dancing partner in *Rosy Rapture*. He did not dance as well as Harry, and their combination on stage lacked sparkle.

The first night that Gaby appeared in *5064 Gerrard*, she joined Robert Hale, already on stage in his 'Gaby' drag, to a tremendous ovation. When the laughter had died down a little she shouted at the audience, 'Which is the real Gaby? How can you tell?' 'By the hat!' screamed a voice from the stalls. Some nights Gaby would find herself almost too helpless with laughter to speak her lines. Years later, Robert Hale's equally talented daughter, Binnie, recalled the impersonation as one of her father's most brilliant.

Gaby found being part of *5064 Gerrard* an enormously rewarding experience after the failure of *Rosy Rapture*. After a shaky start, the summer of 1915 turned out to be one of the happiest she had known. She found a satisfaction in the charity work she was doing that had eluded her in her search for emotional fulfilment. As a public figure, she felt loved. The adulation she received from her audiences more than compensated for the lack of a soul mate. In a way, she had given up the search, and had settled for what she had – which on many levels was a great deal. The two tiny chihuahuas she carried were like the children she had never had. One day, when one of them vanished, she was devastated. The first thing she did was to call Scotland Yard, and then she gave a tearful interview to the *Star*.

'She is so tiny,' wept Gaby, 'such a little thing, her legs no thicker than my finger, with no hair, just like a little r-r-rat. No good to anyone but me. I will offer twenty pounds to anyone that finds her, not because of her value, but because I love her so.'

'You know,' she added, in a tense voice, 'they eat those little dogs in China, they are so delicate . . . and tender. But do not say that in your paper, or someone may eat my Bébé.'

Some days passed. Gaby became more and more unhappy, hardly able to face her nightly appearances at the Alhambra. One night, a shabby-looking man turned up at the stage door and asked to see her. The doorkeeper asked him what he wanted, and out from under his coat popped Bébé. She was a little dirty, but otherwise seemed unscathed.

Gaby was overjoyed, and paid the man his £20 there and then. Bébé had apparently been stolen and sold to a dealer, who hastened to restore the pet to its owner when he read of the reward. The next night she took the whole cast, chorus included, out to dinner by way of a celebration.

Gaby would have been happy to stay on in *5064*, surrounded as she was by so much talent, in a hit show that did fantastic business every night, despite the fact that other revues were opening and closing with alarming rapidity. This was due to a variety of factors, not the least of which was a shortage of young male performers. Lines of forty to fifty-year-old chorus 'boys' were by then a familiar sight in the West End.

Charlot's formula of presenting a revue devoid of any mention of the war had paid off, and was being widely copied. But *5064 Gerrard* was innovative in more than one way. It had a fantastic finale, with the stage completely covered by a large chorus of a hundred pierrots, all wearing identical blonde curly wigs and huge ruffs. Ranged at different levels on the stage, keeping step with great precision, the players created a scene resembling the Busby Berkely film sequences of twenty years later. Gaby was sad to leave, but she had other commitments to honour.

One of the reasons that the names of many of the stars of the music hall became so well-known in the days before broadcasting and film was that they toured the country year after year, not restricting their appearances to London. Their names became associated with certain songs, and with the increasing popularity of gramophone records, an even larger public demanded personal appearances. Gaby had been performing regularly in England for several years by this time, but her appearances had always been restricted to the West End.

Her Triumph was due for release in England, and she wisely chose this time to accept the offer of a tour from the Moss Organization, which had halls the length and breadth of the country. She set off in late July, knowing that she could kill several birds with one stone: as well as publicizing the film, she fully intended to continue her role as a symbol of the Alliance, taking part in recruiting drives, flag days, and as many fund-raising projects as she could fit in. As the tour progressed, she was photographed opening fêtes, giving speeches, and even wearing the ubiquitous full-length chinchilla coat while riding a donkey on Brighton beach, surrounded by wounded soldiers.

Her Triumph had opened in London in June, and was released nationally in September. The openings coinciding in many towns with her personal appearance. It was tremendously well received. Hoardings all over the country pronounced her 'The Sensation of Two Continents'. It had also been released in America, where it did equally well.

Owing to the war, plans that Gaby had laid the previous year to return to the States under the managership of Marinelli had come to nothing. She had subsequently received an offer from one of the top producers in America, Charles B. Dillingham. In August, it was announced that he had signed her to star in the new revue he was planning around a score written by one of the brightest young songwriters around, Irving Berlin. Their previous collaboration had produced a revue called *Watch Your Step*, and from the success this had enjoyed, it was obvious the young Mr Berlin had a brilliant future.

Gaby did not relish the idea of returning to America. But she saw it as a challenge, and was determined to prove, if only to herself, that she could still be a success on Broadway, despite all the flak she had received from critics there. The very fact that Dillingham wanted her proved something. He was, after all, no fool, and had made it quite clear that she would be promoted in a way that would put the Shuberts' handling of her to shame. After seeing her in *Her Triumph*, Dillingham had come to the conclusion that she was by no means a poor actress, and he promised her that his new

118

production would give her a chance to display her talents; to do a little more than just be herself.

After seven weeks on the road, she finished her British tour in Newcastle. On every stop they had made, she had been received rapturously. The Moss management were so pleased with the returns that they signed her to do another tour the following year, at £1,200 per week. Safe in the knowledge that she had this to come back to, whatever happened in America, Gaby went to Paris to organize her costumes for the Dillingham revue. As a famous figure, she encountered less difficulty in obtaining a passage over the Channel than an ordinary civilian would have done.

The war had had a profound effect on fashion. Clothes became much looser, allowing women to fulfil the new activities that were expected of them. The creativity of the designers was, however, in no way impaired – far from it. The new, fuller, freer silhouette allowed limitless possibilities, especially as skirts had become considerably shorter, thus placing much more emphasis on the legs. Soon these newly revealed limbs were decorated with fancy lace stockings, ribbons criss-crossed well up on the calf, or covered by high boots or buttoned spats.

The new fashions found much more favour with the ladies who had to wear them than with the men who had been accustomed to seeing the female form revealed in the tight-fitting styles of the pre-war years. Although Gaby welcomed these looser styles for private wear, on stage their whole effect was less provocative. Thus she found herself in a quandary as to how she could modify the new look for her American tour into costumes that would still be revealing, without making her seem dated. It was not easy. Not that her costumes for America could ever be too risqué. The Puritan streak in American society was still sufficiently strong for the local police chief to have recently insisted that chorus girls at the Winter Garden cover their knees. Gaby decided that, if her costumes had to cover up rather than reveal, they would have to be that much more sumptuous to compensate. If the dresses were to be more modest, the hats would have to be more exaggerated than ever. Each of the vast creations of silk and feathers that she made for the trip needed its own big travelling trunk. Consequently, it was with the staggering total of 180 steamer trunks that Gaby sailed off at the end of October, her face covered by a pink tulle veil, high blue satin boots peeking out from beneath her voluminous chinchilla coat.

Bébé was tucked firmly under her mistress' arm. Waiting reporters in New York noted with joy that the tiny, shivering brute was wearing earrings! Pearls, of course.

14
PRIVATE FEELINGS

Dillingham welcomed her enthusiastically. They had much to discuss. Apart from her forthcoming appearance in his new revue, Gaby's plans for having her own theatre seemed finally to be coming to fruition. Gordon Selfridge had led her to believe that she could count on his backing. Whilst she was in America she would look for a suitable site, and she would discuss with Dillingham whether he might manage this new venture for her.

Her idea of opening a large, American-style theatre in Paris had been curtailed by the war, so she decided to create a small French-style revue house on Broadway. Naturally, the success of Dillingham's new revue would be an important factor in the realization of these plans, but for the moment it was difficult to see how it could possibly fail. His previous offering, *Watch Your Step*, had exceeded all expectations and the new show, *Stop! Look! Listen!*, contained many of the elements that had made its predecessor such a success. Irving Berlin's score contained some of his best material to date, including one number, 'I Love a Piano', that was destined to become an all-time favourite. The talented cast included Harry Fox, and the line-up of beautiful chorus-girls featured Gaby's old friend Marion Davies. Marion's great moment was in a number called 'The Girl on the Magazine Cover'. Joseph Santley sang this song in front of a backdrop consisting of the cover of *Vogue*, while the four gorgeous cover girls came to life★.

The show was a visual feast. Highlights included an incredible set for 'I Love a Piano', consisting of a vast piano running the whole length of the stage. Gaby's big solo spot, 'Everything in America is Ragtime', came in the last act. In it, her skyscraper hats had the

★Years later, when Marion Davies lived with William Randolph Hearst, she gave a large party at San Simeon and restaged this number as a highlight of the evening.

desired effect; several feet of copy in the papers described them as, among other things, 'freakish' and 'nonsensical'.

Stop! Look! Listen! opened in Philadelphia on 1 December to rave local reviews, and transferred to Dillingham's New York base, The Globe, on Christmas Day. On the surface, the revue appeared to be a monumental success, the first week grossing $20,000, the house packed every night. Backstage, however, things were not running so smoothly.

Harry Pilcer was very unhappy with his part in the show. He believed that it should have been much bigger, and that the numbers that Gaby sang with Joe Santley should have been his. He did not believe that Gaby had done her best to persuade Dillingham to give him more to do, and once again fights backstage between Harry and Gaby became a nightly occurrence. By New Year, relations between them had reached an all-time low, and they were not speaking to each other at all.

Gaby was extremely upset, and her performance suffered. She became tense and nervous, and found, for the first time in her life, that she could not forget her personal feelings when the curtain rose. Her voice, never strong, faltered; her acting became stilted and unreal; once or twice she even forgot her lines. She was astonished at Harry's antagonism towards her, but at the same time her innate stubbornness refused to allow her to seek a reconciliation. Her bad performances did not go unnoticed in the press, and her personal reviews grew progressively worse: 'What a great show this would be with a real leading lady,' was their general tone. Needless to say, Dillingham was furious at this turn of events, but he was unable to heal the rift between his two stars, and could do nothing but watch disconsolately as the bad publicity did its work and the weekly takings diminished.

Gaby felt lonely, unloved, and far from home. To her disgust, details of her fights with Harry started to appear in the press. She read that he considered himself to have been greatly instrumental in her success, and that he did not believe he had received sufficient credit. She was shocked to learn that, as far as he was concerned, their partnership was over, and that he intended to enter vaudeville as a double act with his old 'friend' Teddie Gerrard. Worse was yet to come.

Stop! Look! Listen! stumbled on through January and February as audiences steadily declined. Gaby had managed to rally her powers of self-control and put on a brave face despite her unhappiness, but the rot had set in. Company morale was very low, and the friction between Gaby, Harry and Dillingham made itself felt widely. Dillingham closed the show early in March, but Gaby still had four weeks left to run on her contract. He therefore decided to take the production to the Colonial Theatre in Boston for this time, and then to take it on the road with a new, as yet undecided, leading lady.

Gaby was shattered to see how far Harry's animosity towards her could go. In March, as the company arrived in Boston, the papers carried news of the latest vaudeville act to be seen at the Palace Theatre, New York. Harry Pilcer was presenting his sister Elsie together with Gilbert Douglas in a double-act imitating Gaby Deslys. Horrified, Gaby read how Elsie made her entrance 'through a hedge of wistaria, wearing a hooped frock and a grotesquely huge headdress'.

Harry had been the only man she had ever allowed to get close to her and she felt betrayed. Her basic distrust of men had stemmed from her father's early attempts to thwart what she considered to be her destiny, and her mother had reinforced her opinion that any man would try and manipulate her, given the chance. As far as Maman was concerned, Harry was no exception. She had never liked him, and she warned Gaby that Harry was just another man trying to take advantage of her. Gaby had laughed, and said that no man yet had ever got the better of her. Besides, she said, Harry was different, he really cared about her. He was her only true friend.

'You'll see,' Maman had said.

It came as a great blow to Gaby to see her mother's prophecy fulfilled.

Her stay in Boston was one of the unhappiest times of her life. As well as the ghastly business with Harry, she was having to fight off law suits from people who claimed she had broken promises to them and owed them money. Her long-time associate, H.B. Marinelli, who, it will be remembered, had been planning to act as her manager a couple of years earlier, claimed that he had arranged her current contract with Dillingham, and that he was thus entitled

123

to a percentage of her salary. Gaby insisted that she herself had negotiated this contract, and was reluctant to give him a cent. Whatever the truth of the matter, Marinelli and Gaby had been friends for years, and she felt his behaviour was another betrayal.

To make matters worse, she was not in good health. Illness had coincided with personal crises so often that she was beginning to suspect that some of her symptoms were psychologically induced. Consequently, she pushed herself hard, even on days when her body told her she should be resting. Just recently, she had been getting twinges that she felt certain were an early sign of the rheumatism that afflicted her whole family. Her mother, especially, suffered from it badly. It was one of the reasons she had not been accompanying Gaby so much of late, especially when her daughter's trips took her to cold places. She spent more and more time in Marseilles, where the mildness of the winters suited her better. The spring of 1916 had been particularly chilly and late in coming to Boston, and the cold, damp nights did nothing to elevate Gaby's mood. She found herself alone much of the time. She did not feel like company, and particularly did not wish to take up any of the offers that, as usual, were coming her way from various local businessmen and playboys.

She had much time to meditate. She had always been driven by a desperate need to succeed, pulled along by a destiny too powerful to resist. It had dragged her from one city to another, from one scandal to the next. She had got richer and richer, but now for the first time in her life, she questioned why she was doing all of this. Why did she allow fate to pull her headlong through this endless maelstrom of experience? Was she not, after all, the mistress of her own fate? Was she no longer Gaby the powerful, the unmanipulatable, the woman who always got her own way, the freest of spirits? And yet she was being manipulated, by fate and by the position she had created for herself. The realization that she was as powerless to get what she really wanted from life as the next mortal hit her hard.

In the past Gaby had suspected that all her fame and money had stood in the way of her achieving a fulfilling emotional and sexual relationship; she saw now that it had even prevented her from having close friendships. She felt that she had paid dearly for her success.

Being loved by her public was not enough; the image they adored was merely the creation of publicity and had very little to do with the person behind it. She realized she had begun to believe this image herself; how she had lost track of her real self in an effort, albeit an unconscious one, to constantly live up to what her public demanded. She would rather have conducted her life in a quieter way. Certainly, after so many years of excess, her personal taste in clothes tended more and more to understatement. But this was not what her public wanted, so she acceded to their demands: the hats, the furs, the jewels, everything had to be larger than lifesize, bigger and bigger to feed the cravings of the publicity machine that had become an insatiable monster.

One night in Boston, towards the end of this interminable nightmare of a trip, Gaby was sitting in her dressing room in a deeply introspective mood when she received the news from her mother that her father had died. She broke down. She felt herself at the very nadir of her life, unloved and totally alone. Her maid, alarmed, ran to fetch Harry, although he and Gaby had not spoken for weeks. When he came to her dressing room and saw her so totally distressed, his resolve melted, she threw herself into his arms and cried, tears coursing down her pale face, as he cradled her like a child. The curtain went up late that night, but she made her appearance. Harry helped her through it, smiling and giving her encouragement in their scenes together. It was just like old times; by the time the season in Boston came to a close, on 15 April 1916, they were friends again.

The last night was catastrophic. Gaby learned that Marinelli's lawyer was waiting for her at the stage door to serve her with a writ, and she had to stay in her dressing room until after midnight before making her escape out of another exit. However, with Harry back on her side the incident did not seem so bad, and they had laughed and joked in her dressing room, planning how she could escape.

Back in New York, she wanted to leave for France as soon as possible, to sort out her father's affairs. She was not even tempted to stay by an offer from the Palace Theatre to play for one week there for $5,000. Elsie Pilcer's pastiche, which they had recently presented, had apparently whetted their appetites for the real thing.

Her season under Dillingham's management had ended on a very sour note, Dillingham putting the blame for the premature failure of *Stop! Look! Listen!* firmly on her shoulders. Gaby argued that Dillingham had not presented her properly, and did not understand the peculiarities of her public standing. She claimed that he had not publicized the show, or her, in the right way. Eventually, Dillingham withheld a proportion of her salary to settle various claims against her, principally the $6,000 that Marinelli claimed she owed him.

Variety continued its persecution of her in a series of malicious articles, one of which claimed that she meticulously divided up her salary each week, '. . . so much for so much each day. If she had an invitation for a meal the money put aside for that day for food would be put into a "general fund" – this never less than $3,500 and always changed immediately into a draft for Paris'. The source of these so-called facts is not stated, but *Variety* seemed eager to publish anything that would show her in a bad light. They made much of the salaries that Gaby demanded, and got, but at the same time reported, without comment, that Eva Tanguay refused to sign a movie contract unless she was guaranteed $10,000 weekly for three years. That is $1,560,000, a startling sum even now, but a preposterous figure in 1915.

Eager though Gaby was to get herself and Harry out of America, there were still insurmountable stumbling blocks. Because of Harry's Hungarian background, the American government refused to give him a passport as an American citizen. Gaby did her best to help, personally visiting the English and French consulates, but to no avail. When Gaby sailed for London on 1 May 1916, she had to leave Harry behind.

After she had gone, *Variety* lambasted her in a vicious article:

'The Gaby Deslys "boom" lasted a surprisingly long time. Some day an enterprizing statistician will make a compilation of various newspaper booms, and the length of their lives. This will not only be very interesting, but a kind of handbook for the aspiring ones. With facts and figures set relentlessly forth, the boom-mongers will know their bearings. Miss Gabrielle of the Lilies was carried along comfortably for several years.'

The inexplicable grudge that *Variety* held against her was so deep-seated that when she died they did not even give her an obituary.

Gaby stopped briefly in London, en route to Marseilles, where she helped her mother sort out her father's affairs. It was a sad time. Her mother and father had been reconciled before his death and, even though their marriage had not been consistently happy, Maman was grief-stricken. Gaby was relieved that she had managed to see her father, and make her peace with him, at the end of 1914; Maman told her how much that meeting had meant to the old man, and how, as he lay dying, he had talked fondly of his daughter, and had regretted being so hard on her when she was younger. He had never fully recovered from his illness of a couple of years earlier, and had suspected that this sickness might be terminal. As early as May 1914 he had made plans for his death, and reserved a space in the beautiful St Pierre cemetery in the north of Marseilles. Although he had left provision for his burial, Gaby purchased the surrounding plot of land and made arrangements for a large family mausoleum to be constructed of white marble.

After attending to these duties, Gaby left her mother in the hands of Matichon, and made her way back to London. Matichon had achieved her ambition, and had retired from the stage after marrying a wealthy South American businessman, Fernand-Oscar de Conill. In London Gaby received a great welcome. 'Gaby returns with the summer, the flowers, and other bright things,' one newspaper reported. She was glad to be back. Once again, the strong contrast between her treatment by the British press and their American counterparts was much in evidence. In England she was a very popular public figure, widely admired, accepted by society.

Vogue published a feature on her home in Kensington Gore, by then re-christened Montague House, which said 'Riders from the Row cannot miss – nor pass – the gay little house with its leaded windows, its red, red rows of geraniums, and its smart white motor waiting at the door'. The *Tatler* produced a similar article, in the form of a two-page spread of photographs accompanied by a eulogy along the following lines: '. . . one of the most talked-about people in two continents, and an artist who by her dramatic attainment has taken a high place in the Temple of Fame. Mademoiselle Deslys has created a vogue of her own, and is celebrated as the wearer of the most astonishing headdresses that have ever been seen on the stage, together with costumes that are quite *hors concours.*'

Barrie remained a friend, and with Selfridge continuing to supply many of life's material pleasures, it was a happy summer for her. Harry had finally got a visa, and was back in London. There were no immediate plans for work, although she was contracted to do another tour for Moss Empires in the autumn, and was discussing the possibilities of doing a revue for André Charlot the following year.

There was, therefore, much time to socialize, to see and be seen. Gaby became once again a familiar figure around town. Every-where she went she was fêted. *Tatler* noted: '. . . it is funny the way everyone stares at Gaby, isn't it? Though I confess she is well worth looking at.' She was often spotted at the Carlton Grill and at the Piccadilly Hotel, where veteran entertainer Billy Milton recalls seeing her '. . . all feathers and diamonds'. She often went to the theatre, and was particularly interested to see the London version of *Stop! Look! Listen!*, which Alfred Butt had brought over from New York to the Empire. Wimperis and Carrick (who wrote *The Rajah's Ruby* for Gaby in 1914), had written an English version and, under the new title of *Follow the Crowd* – *Stop! Look! Listen!* having already been used in London for another revue – it was the hit of the season.

The revue was by this time an extremely popular form of entertainment, although, due to the idiosyncracies of English licensing laws, it could not be presented as a complete play, but had to form part of a variety bill at theatres which only had a certain type of licence. The English revue had become increasingly lavish in production, and many of its female stars copied Gaby's outrageous mode of dress. A notable example was Teddie Gerrard, who was infamous for the backless dresses she wore. 'Glad to see you're back' remained her most popular song for many years.

Gaby continued her war work in earnest. Every week she assisted in one charity event or another, and she frequently threw open the doors of Montague House and gave lavish teas to parties of wounded soldiers. It was a period of repose for her, and one which she badly needed. She never really rested, however – a busy social life and plans for her forthcoming Moss tour prevented that. As well as designing her own dresses for the tour, the act that she planned was entirely of her own devising. Moss Empires were happy to let her do everything her own way, and no expense was spared. The set was to be an exact replica of Gaby's bedroom and cost £3,000. This entertainment, entitled *Mademoiselle Zuzu*, started its tour at the outer London Moss halls at New Cross, Stratford and Finsbury Park towards the end of 1916, and Gaby's fee of £1,200 per week constituted a record.

15

PUBLIC PROPERTY

The tour of *Mademoiselle Zuzu* continued into the New Year. Gaby returned to London early in 1917. Plans of starring in Charlot's new revue had fallen through, and she had decided to take the monumental step of renting a theatre herself and producing a show with her own money.

After years of wrangling over contracts and percentages, she felt a wonderful sense of independence. She considered that she was experienced enough to run her own show, and although her dreams of having her own theatre had never materialised, this was the next best thing. Through her old friend Alfred Butt, she obtained a lease on the Globe in Shaftesbury Avenue.

Gaby planned to present, not a revue, but a full-length musical comedy, or, as she put it, a 'musical affair'. The work involved would be phenomenal, and despite the fact that she was not in the best of health, Gaby threw herself into the project with gusto. She would be on stage a great deal of the time, and would require many changes of costume. She planned to start out quite plainly dressed, and to gradually work up to more and more elaborate outfits. The music was to be composed by Max Darewski, a young man not yet out of his teens, who had made a great success as a songwriter since he had achieved the position of the 'world's youngest conductor' a few years earlier – at the age of eight.

The revue's working title was *Naughty Suzette* but it opened at the Globe on 29 March 1917 as *Suzette*. It was destined to be Gaby's longest-running show in London, and her last. The opening night was filled with incident. W. McQueen-Pope, at that time manager of the Globe – and later to become one of England's best-known theatrical writers and historians – recalled how Gaby had been barracked when pennies were thrown on the stage.

'The pennies did not come from the gallery. They were thrown by five men in the upper circle who came in of set purpose to make a scene. We were aware of this and could have stopped the men from entering, but Gaby, who knew of it, said that if they wanted to come in they were welcome. I had a force of chuckers-out and policeman in attendance, and we soon had the gentry removed . . .

'. . . Gaby was one of the most genuinely charitable women I have ever met. I never knew her refuse a request for charity. She gave her time and money unsparingly, and worked especially hard for St Dunstan's. Therefore, it is only fair to place on record that her last London venture was an un-qualified success. We opened in March 1917 with *Suzette* and, in spite of the air raids, ran through to October to excellent business.'

He does not, unfortunately, reveal the identity of the group who set out to spoil the first night of *Suzette*, or that of the person who sent them, but the incident ensured that the audience were very much on the side of Gaby and Harry, and when the curtain came down the applause was enthusiastic and prolonged.

The content of *Suzette* was little more substantial than any of Gaby's previous offerings. The action was set in a girls' school in the South of France, with Gaby playing a most unlikely schoolgirl. A fatuous and flimsy plot transformed her into a glamorous nightclub entertainer, performing her familiar acrobatic dances and changing rapidly from one extraordinary costume to another. It is a mystery how she managed so many quick changes, especially as each costume had its own headdress – vast, elaborate structures too far removed from mundane fashion to be called hats. These creations, which had long been Gaby's personal signature, were widely copied, and are still to be seen gracing the few remaining showplaces of spectacular revue, most notably the Folies-Bergère and the Lido in Paris. The London revue stage of 1917 was full of imitations. They were copied directly in a revue called *Smile*, which played at the same time as *Suzette* at the Garrick Theatre. In a scene called, 'With Hats Like Gaby's', Minerva Coverdale appeared wearing a selection of bizarre monstrosities incorporating a dove-cote complete with live doves, birds in their nests, ducks in flight, a whole turkey, and even a pig. Some imitations like Winifred Ellice, who appeared at the Empire in *Hanky Panky*, gave her credit. Others, like Ditty Tarling – surely a name to conjure with! – in *Topsy Turvy* adopted the style as their own.

The sheer beauty of Gaby's costumes for *Suzette* drew nothing but praise. *Tatler* enthused: 'We see Gaby in an amazement of white chiffon and blue Eiffel-towering ostrich feathers, Gaby in a transparency of black and diamonds, Gaby in a conflagration of cerise and gold, Gaby out-Gabying Gaby in each fresh entrance.'

The awful reality of the war seemed to be drawing ever closer. Nightly bombing raids terrorized the population. A wish to forget the privations of daily life drove hordes of people, both civilians and soldiers on leave, into the West End for a couple of hours in which to forget. A note of almost manic cheerfulness is found in the titles of the revues with which they were presented. Apart from the aforementioned productions, others include *Bubbly, Three Cheers, Zig-Zag*, and many in a similar vein. All were designed to transport the audience into a fantasy land of beautiful girls, dazzling costumes and ragtime music. At the Globe, myth and fantasy became reality. Who really cared that the plot of *Suzette* didn't make much sense when they could witness Gaby Deslys swinging on a perch in a vast gilded cage? She was the largest and most spectacular golden canary the world had ever seen.

On the evening of America Day, 20 April, Gaby made an addition to the show, appearing in a dress she had thought up and had made practically overnight. Her body was tightly draped in the English and French flags; her headdress was a high curving arc of red, white and blue striped ostrich feathers, the stars to go with the stripes scattered on the front and forming a halo around the top. She was the symbol of the Allies, and it was her apotheosis.

Gaby's chief dresser at this time was Elizabeth McDonald, an efficient, middle-aged Scotswoman, whose memoirs provide a valuable insight into the character of her employer. 'Mrs Mac' recalls how nervous Gaby was on the first night of *Suzette*. Although not normally afflicted by first-night nerves, this was no ordinary opening. In her first management rôle, she was most anxious that she should be well received. Mrs Mac gave her the sensible advice: 'Just pretend it's the one-hundred-and-first night, M'selle, and everything will be fine'.

Mrs Mac also recalls how Gaby would give her a lift home in her car every night. She recounts a charming story of one night, when the very heavy rain had deterred even the most eager autograph-hunters from waiting outside the stage door. Instead of the usual throng of admirers, just one bedraggled and dirty little girl of about ten or eleven stood outside, huddled up to the wall by the stage door. Gaby saw her before dashing out to her waiting car under an umbrella, and for a moment the little street urchin and the great star stood within a few feet of each other. Gaby turned to the child and said, 'Why do you stand here, little girl? You should be at home'. The little girl said nothing. Mrs Mac, realising that she was tongue-tied, repeated the question. 'I wanted ter see 'er,' she replied, indicating Gaby. Gaby heard her answer, dashed forward, and rushed the astonished child into the big white car. Mrs Mac joined them and heard Gaby say, 'You are a very silly little girl. It is not worth getting a cold, maybe even pneumonia, just to see me. But now that you are here, I will see that you don't suffer for it.' She instructed her chauffeur to drive to a restaurant in Soho where she was well-known.

When they arrived Gaby asked for a private room, and with the manager, head waiter and others dancing attendance, they soon found themselves seated at a supper table. The child could do nothing but stare around her in awe. Gaby requested a towel 'to dry my little friend's hair', and then asked the child what she would like to eat. 'Dunno,' she replied, wriggling awkwardly, and obviously thinking this must be a dream.

The waiter brought a towel, and Gaby herself dried the girl's hair, and gently wiped her rather grimy face before his astonished eyes. From her bag she produced an ivory comb, and tidied the child's hair. 'There,' she said, 'now look how pretty you are.' Slowly, Gaby thawed out her little guest's shyness, and elicited from her the information that she was 'awful fond o' fish an' chips'. Gaby ordered hot soup, and then the child was granted her wish. It was a very different dish of fish and chips from that she was accustomed to – Dover sole with pommes sauté, served with sauce tartare, and cooked by one of the best chefs in London.

It was a strange little supper party, but by the time it was over, the child in her grubby print frock and holed stockings, and the actress in her hundred-guinea evening dress, pearls and diamonds at her throat, were the best of friends. As Mrs Mac listened, she realised that Gaby, in her broken English, and the little girl in her Cockney, were chatting on common ground. Soon Gaby knew all about the little girl's home in Stepney, her brothers and sisters, everything there was to know about her young life.

Instead of going home to Kensington Gore, Gaby made the chauffeur drive out to the East End. During the drive, Gaby had turned to Mrs Mac and said, 'Do you have any money on you, Mac?' Like royalty, Gaby seldom carried ready cash, and frequently borrowed small sums from her dresser. Mrs Mac gave her £2, which she handed to the little girl with the advice that she was to try and save it. In Stepney, Mrs Mac accompanied the little girl into the house to explain to her mother why she was so late. The mother was used to her large family being out at all hours, but thanked her all the same.

This was not an isolated incident. Stories abound of Gaby's generosity. Dr Arthur Bradley recalls an incident from his childhood in 1917;

> 'My family and I lived in St Anne's House, Diadem Court, a small street off Oxford Street. The adjacent flat was occupied by a Mrs Woodings, who was one of Gaby Deslys' dressers at the Globe Theatre. I admired the elegant silks and dresses which Mrs Woodings was ironing one day in her kitchen, and she said it was part of her paid services for the star. She had mentioned on more than one occasion that Gaby was paying for the education of her son at a public school. Also that she generously gave away odd dresses and accessories when used a few times.
>
> 'One day Mrs Wooding asked whether I would like to see the show in which her employer was appearing. She could get me a seat in the "gods" . . . I was thrilled at the prospect, and was ecstatic on seeing the magnificent star complete with her wondrous dresses . . . Mrs Woodings collected me after the show, took me to Gaby's dressing room and introduced us. Imagine the thrill for a boy of ten years old! She spoke to me for a few minutes and I have never forgotten the experience.'

It was a happy time for Gaby, despite the fact that returns at the box office were not wonderful, and that after all the production costs were covered it was unlikely to show her a profit. But that was not the only point of the exercise. What really mattered was that she was finally her own boss; and if *she* was not happy making any money out of her hard work, then at least no one else was.

Matichon had by now gone to live in Syracuse, New York, with her new husband, leaving Maman alone. Gaby invited her mother over to stay with her, and Madame Caire arrived a few days before her sixtieth birthday. Gaby gave her mother many presents on the morning of the special day, and in the evening, when Maman was sitting as usual in her daughter's dressing room, Harry Pilcer's dresser came in with a large bowl of flowers. Mrs Mac took it from him, thinking it was for Gaby, but Gaby called out, 'No, no, it's for Maman'.

'For me? No, it cannot be,' her mother said.

'*Mais oui, Maman*. You know it is your birthday. I know Mac, Maman has her admirer out front, and he has sent these round. Naughty Maman!'

Madame Caire took the bowl and examined the flowers. Then she saw a note amongst them, and she opened it. Inside was a £50 note and a message: 'Une surprise pour Maman – Gaby.'

Mrs McDonald's memoirs also tell us that, despite Alfred Butt's protestations to the contrary back in 1913, Gaby never wore stockings on stage; she always 'wet white' her legs. After particularly strenous dance routines, she would go into the wings and point out to Mrs Mac where the make-up had run. She would put her foot up on a chair, and say, 'Another ladder. Sew it up please, Mac.'

One last amusing incident from the redoubtable Scotswoman's memoirs concerns an interview she had a couple of years later, when Sarah Bernhardt came to London and a British dresser was needed to assist her personal maid:

'An offer was put forward for me to take the job, and I went to see the great tragedienne. The only way I can describe her is that she was exactly like what she had been described as, only more so. I mean that I felt every movement, every gesture and every word she spoke were studied and theatrical. But as soon as I entered the room where she was, I felt also that I was in the presence of a great personality . . . I saw too that she lived like a queen, in the sense that she was accustomed to having her every slightest wish anticipated and obeyed. She asked me who I had been with and amongst others I mentioned Gaby Deslys. She sat up on her couch and broke into a torrent of words which, as they were in her native language, I could not understand. But I got the gist of it from the stage manager who had taken me to see her, after we left. I had said something about the "actress" I had been with. Bernhardt, on hearing Gaby's name, had sat up and hurled forth that it was sacrilege to call Gaby Deslys an actress. She was "a beautiful puppet", a "clothes prop", she was a woman who stood on the stage like an artist's model and showed off her body – but an actress – never!'

Mrs Mac mentions that when she was eventually offered the job, she turned it down: 'Great distinction though it may have been, I had the feeling that working as Sarah Bernhardt's dresser would have been too much for my nerves'.

One night Gaby returned home to Montague House to find it in total disarray. Drawers were half-open, papers scattered. At first she thought she had been robbed. It would have been easy enough to do; her personal maid often accompanied her to the theatre, and she had no other staff that lived in. Maybe someone had been watching her movements . . . But nothing appeared to have been stolen. There was never a great deal of jewellery in the house, it was either on Gaby's person or in the bank*. What little jewellery she had left casually lying about in her bedroom was still there. She thought of calling the police, but on consideration decided not to: there was no point; nothing was missing or damaged. She felt it must have been one of her fans eager to find a memento of his heroine.

* A reporter once asked her, during an interview in her dressing room at the Duke of York's, what she did with her jewellery when she was on stage. She laughingly indicated her maid, who, with a grin, opened her blouse and revealed rows of pearls around her neck. 'Voilà,' said Gaby, 'my walking safe.'

A few days later, one afternoon when she had no matinée, she was at home when her maid announced that two gentlemen were at the door claiming to be from Scotland Yard. The two high-ranking officers were shown in. They were rather embarrassed to ask Gaby if they could see her passport. Gaby, mystified, asked the reason. They told her it was merely a formality, and that they would explain it presently. Gaby produced her passport, which they examined for a while before explaining to her that they were investigating the claims of a Madame Navratil, who had stated in certain continental newspapers that Gaby was her daughter. Gaby laughed. She remembered the woman at the stage door on that night in Vienna, so many years ago. That crazy woman, was she still persisting with her preposterous story?

Scotland Yard did not believe a word of it, but as this was wartime, they had had to investigate such matters. Austria and Hungary were enemies, and if there were any truth to the claims, Gaby would be an enemy alien. They apologized for troubling her and left, telling her that she could expect a further visit from government officials. She was later interviewed by Sir Basil Thompson, who had been instrumental in the bringing to justice of Mata Hari two years previously. He explained to her that there had been reports published in newspapers on the Continent and in America that her real name was Hedwige Navratil, and that she was by nationality Hungarian. Gaby was incredulous: both that there should be any doubt as to her identity (her own mother was in London); and that anyone could possibly doubt her loyalty to the Allied cause. The matter came to nothing, but it left her with an unpleasant after-taste. She was grateful that no mention of it appeared in the British press.

Another drama of a different sort that took place that summer was altogether more amusing, and well-publicized. By now Gaby had become such a legendary figure that her public appearances offstage usually resulted in her being mobbed. News of what she ate, where she went, and especially what she wore was fodder for the tabloids and society press alike, and a scheduled appearance in public was guaranteed to be a major media event. In July 1917, when the news broke that she had been sued by a painter called Ben Olchanevsky for an unpaid debt, and would herself be called as a witness at the hearing, the press men prepared themselves for a field day.

Olchanevsky had been commissioned to paint a portrait of her to be hung in the lobby of the Globe Theatre. Gaby had not liked the result, nor the bill for £20. This was a very small sum, one would think, to a star of her standing – even if it was four or five times the weekly wage of the average working man. But her famed generosity was equalled only by her parsimony if she thought she was being taken for a ride. Moreover, she did not care much for the brash young American painter, and when she told him she did not like the painting, considered it too sketchy amongst other things, and asked if perhaps he might like to do a little more work on it, he refused. In which case, she said, she really did not think the work he had put into it was worth more than £12.

'You should be ashamed of yourself,' he replied, 'making the money you do.'

'If you must know,' she retorted angrily, 'I have not made five pounds since this show opened. I'm only keeping it running so that the cast will not be out of work. Now, if you want your money, you can sue me for it.' Which is exactly what he did.

The case came up on 5 July at the West London County Court. The courtroom was packed. Women had been queuing up outside for seats since the early hours. The scene resembled Oxford Street on the first day of the January sales; this was not something to be missed. When Gaby's familiar white limousine drew up, the crowd eagerly pressed forward. Gasps of delight were heard as she smilingly emerged, magnificently dressed in the black and white she constantly wore in sympathy with the war widows, who had adopted this colour scheme as their unofficial uniform. Her face was pale above the black fox collar of the coat she wore despite the heat; her fair hair almost hidden by a magnificent hat from Maison Lewis, its upturned black brim enclosing deep ruffles of stiff, black organza that towered, quivering, to a good twelve inches above her head. She got to the courtroom with some difficulty; everyone wanted a close-up view of Gaby. Even the presiding magistrate, Judge Selfe, was impressed by the importance of the occasion.

When she was called to the witness box, Judge Selfe asked her why she had refused to pay for the painting. She said it was an absurd portrait, totally unlike her. The picture was produced. It did not seem such a bad likenesss.

'What do you object to?' asked the judge.

'There is much that I object to,' she replied. 'Just look at it. It is not like me one little bit.'

The judge gazed at the portrait, then at his witness. After a slight pause, he said, 'Mademoiselle Deslys, would you be so kind as to remove your hat?'

'Of course,' she said, reaching up her small hands, each one sporting pearl solitaires the size of pidgeons' eggs, to remove the elaborate headgear, which she placed to one side of the witness box. Fluffing up the tawny blonde curls that had been flattened by the hat, she smiled her irresistible smile at the elderly judge, and asked, 'Is that better?'

He smiled back. 'Much better, Mademoiselle,' and continued the comparison. After a few moments he asked her, in a gentle voice, 'What *exactly* do you object to? I personally find it not a bad likeness.'

'The whole thing is wrong. It is just not me.' By now, she was a little flushed and excited. 'It is just not me,' she repeated. 'It is wrong in the . . . the . . . how you say, in the *ensemble*.'

The judge remained unconvinced. Despite the claim of Gaby's lawyer that the portrait had been painted as a speculation, not a commission, judgement went against her, and she was ordered to pay the full amount plus costs. Gaby bowed solemnly to the judge and followed the painting out of the courtroom and through the milling crowds to her car. She was furious. The gentlemen of the press crowded around, eager for her to say a few words about her defeat. She turned to a reporter and asked, 'Do you by any chance have a penknife?' Mystified, he obliged. Holding the knife, she gave them the speech they were waiting for.

'I suppose I must pay,' she said through clenched teeth, 'But I feel I must in some way show my appreciation of this work of art.' As the cameras clicked, she raised the knife and slashed at the picture until only a few shreds of canvas hung from the frame.

It was indeed true that she was making no money out of *Suzette*, but there were compensations. She adored being her own boss and running a theatre. As part of her war effort she lent the theatre out for charity galas, to the Home Camps Concert Fund in June, to the Irish Women's Association in July; and she gave charity performances of *Suzette*, the takings from which went directly to one or other of her pet causes. Her car was at the disposal of the whole company; she even lent it to a chorus girl on the occasion of her marriage to a soldier on leave. Her generosity as a boss as well as a friend became part of her myth.

As for the future, she had no direct plans. Following the success of *Her Triumph* she was eager to make another film, and had been considering several offers, but ultimately none had proved interesting enough. For the time being, her life had some routine, and proceeded at a comparatively leisurely pace. She worked hard as usual at the theatre, opened fêtes and bazaars for numerous charities. At a Theatrical Garden Party in aid of the Actors' Orphanage, held in the grounds of Chelsea Hospital, she raffled her 'secret' – or, as she put it, '*ce qu'il faut pour être aimé*' – which consisted of a single lump of sugar in a little silk bag, and raised the then staggering sum of £168. At 1s. a ticket, that represented many sales. The crowd around her stand was dense from the minute she appeared.

Crowds of onlookers also had to be held back on another occasion, when she posed for publicity shots in Kensington Gardens with a flock of sheep, dressed as Marie Antoinette. Her popularity was such that a host of teashops, hatshops and hairdressers were named after her; one such hairdressers, situated off Bond Street, took her profile as its logo, and survived until the 1950s. An enterprizing Oxford Street trader also conceived the idea of opening a glove shop called Gaby's near to Selfridges. Gordon Selfridge himself got to hear of the plan, and for some reason found the idea objectionable. He managed to persuade the trader to change his mind, but the persuasion proved expensive.

This most pleasant period in her life came to an abrupt end with the appearance in London, under the most remarkable circumstances of a friend from Paris, Jacques-Charles. Jacques-Charles had

known Gaby from her earliest days in Paris. As her star ascended, his career too had blossomed. The young man that she had originally met at the Mathurins had graduated from drawing cartoons to writing a theatrical gossip column for *Gil Blas*, then to working as a press agent. He became general secretary to the Isola Brothers, who controlled not only the Parisiana, the small music hall where Gaby had obtained her first job, but also the Folies-Bergère and the Olympia. When they planned to take over the Paris Opéra, they made a gift of the Olympia lease to Jacques-Charles, the reason for this apparent magnanimity being that the lease was virtually unsaleable. The Olympia was a comparatively small hall in a very expensive neighbourhood, and the high rent made it a difficult theatre to run at a profit. Jacques-Charles was undeterred. It gave him the opportunity of fulfilling a lifetime's ambition of writing and staging his own revues. A hard worker, he proved to be a gifted impresario, personally overseeing every detail of his productions. The venture was a great success, and by the time war broke out he had obtained the lease of his second theatre, the Marigny.

At the outbreak of the war, all places of amusement in Paris had been closed. Only after the Battle of the Marne had been won by the French towards the end of September 1914, so saving Paris from German occupation, did the theatres and music halls slowly re-open, but business was very poor. So many artists had been conscripted that it was difficult for the managers to find good acts to book. The paying public, too, had been depleted by conscription, and those that were left were in no mood for frivolity.

Fortunes were lost, among them that of Jacques-Charles. He too had gone off to fight at the Front, and after facing death and enduring what seemed like an eternity of cold and unspeakable squalor in the trenches, he had ended up seriously injured in a military hospital late in 1916. Here he was visited by an old friend, Léon Volterra. Volterra was one of the very few men who had actually profited from the disastrous effect the war had had on the Paris music hall. He had always been a remarkable opportunist.

As a small child of seven or eight, Volterra had been abandoned by his parents, and had made his way up in the world by a series of ingeniously thought-out frauds. Streetwise in the extreme, his earliest money-making venture involved picking old newspapers out of dustbins, re-folding them, and selling them as 'the latest news'. This he accomplished cleverly disguised as a newsboy, complete with a large canvas bag, and a fertile imagination that enabled him to invent sensational news items, which he would cry out to tempt prospective readers. By the time they realized they had bought yesterday's paper, he would be streets away.

His next ruse was more elaborate, but far more rewarding. He used to loiter around the streets of the flower market at Les Halles, picking up broken blooms, attaching the heads to wire stems, and arranging them into tight little bouquets. He then went to one or other of the many fairgrounds in Paris where he kept a close eye on courting couples. When one of the girls left her beau to take a ride on a roundabout, he too would climb on and present a bouquet to her, shouting above the noise, 'M'sieur has bought you these flowers'. The delighted girl, by now riding round and round on a golden horse, would wave and smile lovingly at her man. This was Léon's cue to leap off the roundabout and approach the gentleman, saying, 'M'selle has bought a bouquet'. Thus he would elicit a few francs. Other ruses Volterra adopted included selling in the markets 'pairs' of shoes that had two left feet, and opening the doors of limousines as they pulled up outside theatres. This was his introduction to the theatre, a world he grew to love. He had ended up selling programmes at the Olympia, when it was under Jacques-Charles' control, and they had become friends.

When Jacques-Charles opened his Palais de Danse, Léon persuaded him to let him have sole control of the sale of programmes. Jacques-Charles had protested that there was no need of programmes: 'The orchestra plays, the customers dance,' he said. But Volterra insisted that he had clients, perfumiers and sweet manufacturers, who would pay advertising charges, irrespective of how many programmes were sold. Reluctantly, Jacques-Charles let Volterra have his way, and by the end of the season the enterprise had paid off. Volterra had made 5–6,000 francs which became the basis of his fortune.

After war broke out and the music halls had closed, Volterra went into business with Raphael Beretta, musical director of the Olympia and, paying a concession to Jacques-Charles and the building's proprietors, he made this hall one of the first to re-open after the Battle of the Marne. With so little competition this first season went well, and the following year, in Jacques-Charles' absence, Volterra and his associates bought control of the Olympia. This was followed the next year by the purchase of the Folies-Bergère and Les Ambassadeurs, and finally the Casino de Paris. By 1917 Volterra had fallen out with his associates, and they bought out his interest in the business for one million francs.

It was at this time that Volterra went to see Jacques-Charles in the military hospital. He explained that he had secretly bought the Casino de Paris from his old associates for next to nothing, using the name of one of his relatives, as Beretta would have been reluctant to let him have it.

The Casino had done very badly in the war; several owners had tried to make it pay, but one by one they had fallen bankrupt. Beretta had begun to see it as a liability, and was eager to cut his losses and get rid of it. Volterra, on the other hand, was delighted to get hold of the lease, and planned to re-launch the Casino as a serious rival to the Folies-Bergère. This, he felt, would teach his ex-associates a lesson. He proposed to Jacques-Charles that they become partners in this venture: Volterra would supply the theatre and the money, his friend would contribute his considerable expertise as a producer.

Jacques-Charles needed time to think and told Volterra to come back in a few days. A week or so later, having given it much thought, he decided to fall in with Volterra's plan. However, although he was eager to get back to work, he still felt weak, and needed time to convalesce. He told Volterra that he would spend a few more months in bed, but that he would use the time to write a new revue.

'Make it something really sensational,' Volterra told his friend, 'and while you're doing that, I'll start work on the Casino.' He had ambitious plans for the Casino de Paris; plans that would transform it into the most modern and luxurious music hall in Paris.

Jacques-Charles came out of hospital and started writing the new revue. He and Volterra had frequent conferences, and eventually the script was completed to their mutual satisfaction. Volterra was more than happy with it, but told Jacques-Charles that the conversion of the Casino had cost much more than he had anticipated, and was nowhere near complete. It was therefore vital that they find someone to star in the revue who could absolutely guarantee its success. Jacques-Charles thought of Gabys Deslys. He knew she had taken her own theatre in London, and that her show there, *Suzette*, had been running for five months, to all appearances very successfully.

'You know,' said Jacques-Charles to Volterra, 'a few years ago, soon after Gaby's name had been associated with King Manuel and the Portuguese revolution, I was in London at the same time as she was, and helped her mother nurse her through a serious illness. Gaby was very grateful, and told me that if ever I needed a favour from her I only had to ask.' Volterra, whilst agreeing that Gaby would be perfect for the revue, doubted that she would agree to do it. Jacques-Charles said they had nothing to lose by going to London to find out.

In July 1917 they managed to board a boat of homeward-bound English soldiers, Jacques-Charles in his army uniform and Volterra in a similar one loaned from a theatrical costumier. They eventually arrived at the Savoy, and after a much-needed bath, rest and change of clothes, presented themselves at the stage door of the Globe, getting there just before the evening performance. The scene backstage was the usual panic before the curtain went up, stage-hands, chorus girls and dressers rushing in every direction. Madame Caire happened to be coming in at the same time and, recognizing Jacques-Charles, fell into his arms and led the two surprise visitors to her daughter's dressing room. Gaby, too, was delighted to see her old friend after so long. Jacques-Charles presented her to Volterra.

'You don't mind if I carry on with my make-up? The half-hour has been called, and I can't be late.' As she sat down before her mirror, Jacques-Charles briefly outlined the reason for their visit.

'But it's impossible,' she said, 'I have taken this theatre at my own expense, and I had planned to run the show right through the winter. And anyway, no one in Paris could pay me what I'm making here.'

Jacques-Charles showed her the contract Volterra had drawn up in advance, on which they had stated the maximum they could pay her. He told her that the war had ruined him.

'I've nothing left,' he said, 'not a penny. I've lost my two theatres, the Marigny and the Olympia. After three years of war and six months in hospital, I have to try and put my life back together. Do you remember years ago, when you told me that if ever I needed anything, I only had to ask? Well, now my need is desperate. Will you help me?'

There was a long silence, broken only by the call boy's knock and cry of, 'Fifteen minutes, Miss Deslys'. Gaby put the finishing touches to her lipstick, and eventually said, 'Go out front and watch the show, then tomorrow come to lunch at the house and I'll give you my reply'.

She had much to think about. She did not want to leave London. But irrespective of what she had told Jacques-Charles, she was not making money out of *Suzette*, and there were no other offers on the horizon. That night, after the show, she discussed the matter with Maman. The next day, she greeted Volterra and Jacques-Charles at Montague House, and gave them a guided tour before lunch. No mention was made of their proposition, and as they went in to the dining room Volterra whispered in Jacques-Charles' ear, 'It's no good, she's going to say no'.

They sat down, and as Jacques-Charles unfolded his napkin, he found inside it the contract he had left with Gaby the night before. At first he did not dare inspect it, but then he looked up to see Gaby and Madame Caire both smiling. He opened the contract and saw, to his relief, Gaby's bold signature at the bottom. He was touched to see that she had also added a clause which read: 'The artist will herself pay for her dancer, Mr Harry Pilcer, her personal costumes, and those of the girls in her scenes'. It was a wonderful gesture, and Jacques-Charles was touched. There was a tear in his eye as he said, 'Thank you. It is a beautiful way of showing your friendship.'

The next few weeks were busy ones for Gaby. She was never happier than when there was a new project afoot. Her stay in London had been so prolonged that a move would necessitate a

Publicity shot, 1917

Gaby in London, Summer 1917. The pearls she is wearing would be priceless now

A skit on Gaby from the Alhambra revue *Keep Smiling*, 1913. The big box contains 'A hat for Gaby Deslys', the small parcel one of her dresses

From *Suzette*, 1917

Publicity shot, 1913

Finale of *5064 Gerrard*, Alhambra Theatre, 1915

With Signoret in the movie *Bouclette*. It was filmed in 1918

Gaby Deslys, *circa* 1915

On stage at the Casino de Paris, 1918. Photograph by Jacques-Henri Lartigue

Gaby with Harry Pilcer, filming *Le Dieu du Hasard*, summer 1919. Photograph by Jacques-Henri Lartigue

Number 3 Rue Henri de Bornier

The Villa Gaby, near Marseille

Gaby, during the last year of her life

Gaby's tomb in Marseille

great deal of planning. She was reluctant to bring *Suzette* to a close, as this would put so many performers and technicians out of work, but she planned to take many of the chorus with her. For some of these young girls it was to be their first visit abroad, and an exciting venture. Jacques-Charles supervized the drawing-up of their contracts, and had to teach Volterra how to write, 'Read and approved' at the bottom of them. It was remarkable that this shrewd and successful businessman had never learnt to read or write.

Gaby had no idea how long she would be out of the country; all would depend on the success of the new venture. The party she gave for the cast after the last night of *Suzette* in early October was prolonged by sad farewells, Gaby often remarking, 'I daresay I will be back before long'. The show had run for 256 performances, her longest time in any production. In some ways she was apprehensive about once again working under contract to someone else. She knew that she could get along with Jacques-Charles, but Volterra was an unknown quantity. She liked him well enough on first sight, but her deep-seated distrust of all men, especially theatrical impresarios, prevented her from becoming very friendly with him. She liked, however, the fact that he appeared to be down-to-earth, a straightforward individual who did not mince his words. Jacques-Charles' obvious admiration for his partner was also a great reassurance.

Her friendship with Gordon Selfridge seemed to have run its course. Gaby knew that a long separation would probably mean the end of it. She did not feel any great sadness. Their friendship had been a mutually convenient arrangement, and after approximately four years the novelty had worn off for both of them. The previous year, 1916, Selfridge had moved his family out of London to Highcliffe Castle in Hampshire, which he rented for £5,000 a year. Since then his meetings with Gaby had become less frequent. In 1918, only months after Gaby's departure, Selfridge's wife died of pneumonia, leaving him free to squander his fortune on a succession of beautiful show-business mistresses. The most notable of these was Jenny Dolly, who he met in 1923 with her sister Rosie at the Kit-Kat Club. His friendship with Jenny was long lasting, but her passion for emeralds was eventually instrumental in Selfridge losing control of the store he had founded.

GD-6

Harry's Hungarian background once again caused difficulties, and he could not get a French visa. Gaby promised him that she would do what she could in France, and then in October 1917 she sailed, accompanied by her mother. She did not realize that she would never see England again.

16

LET 'EM FALL!

In Paris, Volterra and Jacques-Charles had been encountering many difficulties. Volterra's rise had been a rapid one, and on his way up he had made many enemies. His ex-partners were especially angry with the way he had taken control of the Casino, and were determined to put as many obstacles in his way as they could. The news that Gaby Deslys had been engaged for the opening revue had caused a stir in the theatre world, and Volterra's enemies became determined to ruin the production. Workers busy on the conversion of the Casino had been harassed, but this was only the beginning.

Jacques-Charles and Volterra were crestfallen to see Gaby arrive alone, but she was full of confidence that Harry could get his visa as soon as verification arrived from New York that he was a naturalized American citizen. This, in time, came through. But when Harry arrived in France he was arrested by the American authorities there as a draft-dodger, and was told he would be impelled to join the American forces. Volterra and Jacques-Charles were certain that their enemies, especially Volterra's ex-associates at the Folies-Bergère, were to blame for this, but it was a mystery how they had accomplished it. No less of a mystery was the way Gaby managed to solve the problem and get Harry released.

She took up residence at 3, rue Henri-de-Bornier, and all her days – and many of her nights – were taken up with the new show. As Paris was being bombed with increasing frequency, the show's title *Laissez-les Tomber!*, or *Let 'em Fall!*, seemed remarkably apt. The show had been planned on a massive scale, and was in many ways to become a milestone in theatrical history. The sets, the costumes, the music were all exceptional. The cast of 300 artists included a chorus line of 150 beautiful girls. After three years of war, Parisians were starved of luxury and glamour, and Jacques-Charles planned to give them a real feast.

To accommodate the huge audiences they anticipated, Volterra had built a new circle on the cantilever system. His enemies had informed the authorities that this was an unsafe structure, and he was visited by officials who told him they feared for its soundness, and that vigorous tests of the balcony's strength would have to be made. These tests consisted of loading the circle with bags of sand equivalent to ten times the weight of any audience it could possibly seat. It took hours to carry the load up, and it was midnight before it was in place. Volterra spent the night in a chair seated underneath the circle. When Jacques-Charles went back in the morning, he was relieved to find the structure intact. Volterra told him, 'You would never have seen me again if the balcony had fallen. Me and my fortune would have been buried together.'

As a precautionary measure, the Préfecture decreed that two large wooden pillars be built as extra support. They survived as a fixture of the building right up to its closure over fifty years later. Jacques-Charles wrote:

> 'From that day on, rehearsals took place on the stage of the Casino to the sound of the pillars being constructed. The heating wasn't working, so a brazier was lit on the stage and the safety curtain dropped. When we needed to judge the effect of the costumes against the scenery the curtain was lifted for a moment. One saw for an instant, picked out by a spotlight, the pale flesh of the players, frozen by the winds coming into the hall, which was open to the weather.'

The whole operation cost a fortune, and eventually used up every penny Volterra had. One day, he gave 100 francs to a dancer whose husband had just been killed at the Front, and whispered to Jacques-Charles, 'That was my last hundred francs'. Without Gaby's financial assistance, the venture could never have taken off.

Despite all the set-backs and delays, Gaby's faith in the revue never faltered. She received anonymous 'phone calls telling her that Volterra was bankrupt, which she already knew, and that the building might collapse – everything to put her off the venture. But she thrived on adversity, was as determined as anybody to get the show on, and used her considerable powers to make *Laissez-les Tomber!* the most widely anticipated theatrical event in years.

Her enthusiasm was unbounded. She designed and supervized the making of costumes for herself and her 'girls', and as usual worked tirelessly to get her dance routines perfect to the last step. The only part of the show about which she had any reservations was one scene that Jacques-Charles called, 'The Ladders Tableau'. For this scene, twelve ladders thirty feet high were ranged across the stage, and down these would descend, one by one, dozens of beautiful chorus girls, naked except for G-strings, high heels and vast feather headdresses. When Gaby first saw this set she told Harry, 'He must have gone crazy in the war'.

Perhaps the most exciting feature of the revue was the music. Harry Pilcer's brother, Murray, had come over from New York, bringing with him a jazz band, in which he played the drums. It would be the very first time that a real American jazz band had played in Europe, pre-dating the appearances of the Original Dixieland Jazz Band that would revolutionize popular music in the 1920s.

When *Laissez-les Tomber!* finally opened, it was a sensation. The audience went wild with enthusiasm from the minute Gaby first appeared, posed under a huge apple tree in full bloom looking, as a reviewer later said, 'like a petal blown down in waltz time', through to the frenzied dance routines accompanied by a band that featured wailing saxophones and revolvers firing blank ammunition. The breathtaking audacity of 'The Ladders Tableau', with one beautiful girl after another descending the ladders, until the huge stage of the Casino was covered in an undulating mass of sequins, feathers and flesh moving in time to the jazz rhythms, was almost too much for people to take in.

A dream sequence, beautifully executed by dancers draped in black and white chiffon, the spotlights piercing the sheer fabric to reveal their nudity underneath, lulled the audience into a reverie, soon exploded by Gaby and Harry wildly jazzing up and down a vast staircase, that seemed to have materialized at the back of the stage from nowhere. It was an exciting, emotional evening. The curtain fell to applause as crazed as the music; Gaby took one curtain call after another, dragging a modestly reluctant Jacques-Charles up onto the stage to share in her glory.

Paris was packed with American soldiers and officers. Always more demonstrative in their appreciation than Europeans, they screamed, whistled and cheered the show night after night, month after month. Jean Cocteau described the scene one night:

> '. . . Mr Pilcer, in tails, thin and rouged, and Mlle Gaby Deslys, like a big ventriloquist's doll with a porcelain complexion, corn-coloured hair and a gown of ostrich feathers, danced to this hurricane of rhythm and drumbeats of a kind of domesticated cataclysm which left them completely drunk and dazzled under the streaming glare of six air-raid searchlights. The house stood and applauded, roused from its torpor by this extraordinary number, which is to the frenzy of Offenbach as a tank is to an 1870s state carriage.'

The critics were almost unanimous in their praise of the music, the sets, the costumes and, most of all, Gaby. Her costumes with headdresses 'too big to pass under the door of Notre Dame', were universally admired. The jazz score, however, was a little too much for one or two more staid reviewers, one of whom described *Laissez-les Tomber!* as a revue 'suitable only for the deaf and dumb'. Another said: 'Thanks to Gaby Deslys, Paris is Paris once more.' With *Laissez-les Tomber!* the spectacular revue had reached its highest point, and had achieved a form that would be the basis for such revues for decades to come. The awe-inspiring sets, the towering headdresses, the vast – sometimes nude – chorus; the jazz music; the whole thing being built around a glamorous female star, or *meneuse*, clad in a dramatic flurry of feathers and sequins; all this set the style for subsequent revues at the Casino de Paris, which were universally copied for decades to come. Gaby Deslys paved the way for Mistinguett, then, later, for Josephine Baker, and generations of female entertainers noted for their ostentatious presentation. The style has perpetuated to the present day, and is visible in the stage performances of, for example, Diana Ross.

As 1918 progressed, German raids on Paris became more frequent. Nobody realized that peace was only months away. The enemy seemed to be getting closer and their Gotha bombers pummelled Paris in stupefying bombardments. The tension before each performance became almost tangible. If the air-raid sirens sounded before ten o'clock, the audience had to have their money refunded, and each show became a race against time. This was particularly so for the cast, who knew that, if the audience was reimbursed, they would not be paid. On more than one occasion the sirens went off half-an-hour or twenty minutes before the curtain was due to come down, and the delirious crowd and cast just carried on. It really was a case of 'Let 'em Fall!'

If the sirens sounded in the middle of the show, everyone had to evacuate the theatre as quickly as possible. Theatres were all allocated specific shelters. The Casino audience went to the two nearest Métro stations; the cast to the basement of the fire station in nearby rue Blanche. Jacques-Charles recorded the scene there:

> 'Naturally, as the sirens let out their sinister wail, everyone fled exactly as they were, without taking off costumes and make-up. The cellars of the fire station often presented a picturesque scene. All the ladies of the chorus, very hurriedly dressed, having only had time to throw a coat over their shoulders, were side-by-side with the firemen, their wives in curlers, and their kids. At first the atmosphere was a little cold, but little by little relations thawed out. The showgirls at this time were nearly all married, their soldier lovers having married them so they could benefit from a pension if they were killed in action. Many were already mothers, a factor which broke the ice. The firemen's wives at first let the girls make a fuss of their children; then they could sympathize with the worries of motherhood.

Soon the firemen's wives were asking the girls to bring their children to the station before the shows, in order that they would know where their sons and daughters were when the alert went, and would not have to worry about them. Jacques-Charles noted that, 'The shelter resembled a crèche where bizarrely made-up and costumed mothers came to feed their babies in the interval, when the show was not disturbed by Germans.'

The bombing raids did little to suppress Parisian café society, though they did mean that by necessity some of its favourite haunts would have to move underground. For example, a plush and splendid air-raid shelter, the cellars of the Hotel Edward VII, became the 'in' nightspot, where the theatrical aristocracy of 1918 rubbed shoulders after the sirens had sounded. Volterra was to be found there drinking in the company of Mistinguett, her frequent stage partner Maurice Chevalier, and others.

Gaby was more often to be found in the basement of the fire station, where the firemen's wives began to discover something that the chorus girls had known for some time. Beneath her paint and feathers, her pearls and diamonds, lay a warm, unaffected human being. The children adored her. Jacques-Charles said that they must have regarded her as their fairy godmother, so often did she appear loaded down with toys and sweets. She and Harry would play tirelessly with them, Harry down on all fours to give them rides; he was like a child himself. As the year wore on the raids got more severe, more frequent. To Volterra's intense irritation, hardly a night went by when the show was not interrupted by the sirens.

After months of this exhilarating, if nerve-racking, nightly routine, Gaby informed Volterra in April 1918 that she and Harry needed a break. There were few stars in Paris of sufficient stature to take their places, but two possibilities were Mistinguett and Maurice Chevalier. Volterra approached them, and despite Mistinguett saying that they never appeared in revues not specially written for them, *Laissez-les Tomber!* was such a smash hit that they agreed to do it. Mistinguett had been appearing at the Folies-Bergère, and Volterra was delighted to rob his ex-partners of their biggest attraction.

Mistinguett was born Jeanne Bourgeois in 1875, and by the time she was twenty years old she had established a reputation as a singer and comedienne of great talent, portraying low-class women in various Paris music halls. She first worked with Chevalier, who was thirteen years her junior, at the Folies-Bergère in 1909, where their well-publicized romance and stage partnership started. 'Miss', as she was popularly called, was known to be very possessive of her young lover, who had a reputation as a highly sexed ladies' man. They both knew Gaby Deslys well. They moved in the same circles, although Gaby was a much bigger star. Mistinguett had to wait until she was well into her forties before coming into her own as the queen of the Paris music hall. Chevalier's career spanned eight decades. He eventually conquered Hollywood, thereby becoming the most widely known 'music hall star' of all time.

Curiously enough, Chevalier hardly mentions Gaby in his biographies. Mistinguett does, but scathingly. In *Mistinguett and her Confessions*, a series of interviews with Hubert Griffith, she remembers Gaby as having 'no talent in the exact sense', and as being more 'gentille' than beautiful. In her autobiography, *Queen of the Paris Night*, her antipathy is more pointed. She states that *Laissez-les Tomber!* was 'the birth of the music hall as we now know it', but neglects to mention that the revue was written around Gaby Deslys, and not herself. She also hints at having had an affair of some sort with Harry Pilcer. She wrote: 'Though it is true that I never imitated anyone, this did not prevent me from eyeing what Gaby Deslys bought, and buying what she had her eye on. It began with her chemises in the rue de Douai, and ended up with her dancing partner. He caught my eye when I first set eyes on him, pretty much as he had caught hers in New York.' She relates with some relish that Harry had at first found Gaby sexually uninteresting, a fact that she could only have found out from Harry himself.

The only other mention that Mistinguett makes of Gaby in her autobiography is in repetition of an apocryphal story originally published in Michel Georges-Michel's memoirs, *Une Demi-siècle de Gloires Théâtricales*:

> 'The most famous of her lovers was Manuel of Portugal, who lost his crown for her, so they say. However, there is a story that Manuel put in an appearance at a restaurant where Gaby Deslys was dining with a party of friends. Gaby turned white. "What do I do now?" she muttered, "We've never even met. They're going to call my bluff."
> Manuel walked calmly over to the table and addressed one of the party.
> "Will you introduce me to Mademoiselle Deslys?" he said, "I should be happy to ratify this most entrancing of falsehoods." '

It is curious that Mistinguett should choose to remember Gaby Deslys in her memoirs almost solely with this story, not even correctly quoted, and designed to undermine Gaby's legendary status. It is, after all, unlikely that Gaby would have risked libel by making the statements that she did regarding her friendship with the King.

Mistinguett never gave Gaby credit for the tremendous influence she had on her own style and presentation. The cabaret style that made her such a big star in the 1920s for example, was a direct copy of Gaby's. Even the reviewers of Mistinguett's version of *Laissez-les Tomber!*, which opened in May 1918, noticed the similarity between the two women. One critic said: 'She has out-Gabied Gaby'.

Why did Mistinguett dislike Gaby so intensely? Perhaps the answer lies in a telegram preserved in the archives of the Theatre Museum. It is dated 11 September 1911, and in it Gaby writes to Alfred Moul from Paris telling him that she will be in London the following week to discuss her 1912 season. She says: 'I will have with me Monsieur Chevalier of the Folies-Bergère'. Programmes for the Folies-Bergère that year reveal only one Chevalier on the bill – Maurice. Did Gaby Deslys have an affair with Mistinguett's wayward young lover? An affair Mistinguett would never forgive her for? Was she planning to take Chevalier as her stage partner? In 1911, Gaby Deslys, in the wake of the Manuel affair, was by far the biggest name on the Paris music hall stage, and any up-and-coming young entertainer would have been delighted to boost his career by becoming her partner. Perhaps Gaby had made Chevalier this offer, and in the meantime had gone off to America, only to come back with Harry Pilcer, thereby inciting Chevalier's life-long resentment. Only Mistinguett or Chevalier would be able to say for sure what happened, and it is too late to ask either.

Jacques-Charles wrote in several new numbers for Mistinguett and Chevalier, and this second version of *Laissez-les Tomber!* ran on into the summer months of 1918.

As the long summer break and traditional time for the closure of the theatres approached, Volterra hit on a new idea. When the theatres re-opened in the autumn, he would take the original version of the revue to Marseilles, leaving the second running in Paris. He knew that the population of Marseilles had tripled since the war began. The city was crammed with Parisians fleeing the air.

raids, and, as the centre of the Eastern Expeditionary Force, it was also filled with servicemen of every nationality. These newcomers formed a vast new public, eager for diversion and entertainment. Volterra had heard that the service industries in Marseilles had been making huge profits, and he wanted a slice of the action.

On 18 August Volterra arrived in Marseilles, and began looking for a suitable theatre. He soon found it. The old Chatelet Theatre in the Allées de Meilhan had had a chequered career. It had been a popular music hall in its time; Polin, Fragson and other big names had played there. But it was a very large hall, and despite several changes of management and name (it had been the Apollo Theatre, and more recently the Café Martino, and then a boxing stadium), no one had made it a paying proposition. Encouraged by his success with the Casino de Paris, Volterra purchased the lease extremely cheaply, and set about organising a vast army of workers to transform it into a modern music hall. He went back to Paris and confronted Jacques-Charles and Gaby with his *fait accompli*.

Meanwhile, Gaby had not been idle. When she came out of the show in May, instead of taking the break she needed and deserved, she had spent a few weeks making her second film. She had been approached by the French producers Mercanton and Hervil in the summer of 1918, with a script based on Marcel l'Herbier's novel *L'Ange de Minuit* which had been translated into English as *The Angel of Forgiveness*. Although the story seems trite and predictable now, Gaby considered that the strong central character was a very suitable one for her to portray. Once again, she was required to be a little flower girl, alone and starving in her garret, with no one but her little poodle for company. Soon however, she metamorphoses into a glamorous cabaret star, thanks to the much older actor who has fallen in love with and married her. But success goes to her head, and she soon ditches her redeemer for a handsome, rich, titled playboy. Of course, no good comes of their liaison, and the end of the movie finds our heroine reunited with her broken-hearted husband and adorable poodle.

Encompassing, as it did, the mixture of pathos and glamour that Gaby could so easily evoke, the central rôle was tailored to her talents. With Signoret, a renowned character actor, as her husband; Harry as the debonair playboy; and Snowball the poodle as himself, the whole project was a great succes. Although details of her contract are not known, it seems likely that Gaby had a hand in the production at executive level.

The film was released the following year under its original title of *Bouclette* in France, *Gaby* in Great Britain, and (by Pathé) *Infatuation* in the United States. It showed Gaby at her best. The tragedy is that, in 1986, no complete prints of it, or of her two other feature films seem to have survived.

When Volterra came back from Marseilles with his news of the new theatre, Gaby was thrilled with the idea, and fell in with the plan at once. Jacques-Charles set about rewriting the script, introducing, with Gaby's help, jokes and topics that would appeal to a local audience. Volterra told them that the Grand Casino, as he had decided to call his new theatre, would be ready by mid-October, and he wanted the whole company to be moved to Marseilles by then.

Gaby and Maman prepared to make the move south. Although she had made a few trips back over the years, Gaby had never played her home town. She decided to go down ahead of the company to look for a suitable house to rent.

17

THE LADDERS
OF VICTORY

Gaby's joy at being back in Marseilles was indescribable. Asked by
local reporters what it was like to come back after such a long
absence, she said: 'Whenever I am playing in some foreign theatre,
always present in my mind's eye and in my heart is my beautiful
city of Marseilles. Returning here is like coming into the sun after
years in the dark'. She began house-hunting immediately, for she
planned to stay quite a while.

The last few years, spent in London and Paris in an atmosphere of
cold and danger, had taken their toll. Her rheumatism had been
terrible over the winter, her bones ached even as she thought about
it. And sometimes, she had even begun to feel old. She would be
celebrating her thirty-seventh birthday just before the show
opened. Of course, that was not her official age, but a secret she
shared with Maman and her sister. She planned to give a big party
for the cast, her family and old friends, and she needed to find a
house quickly.

So many people had moved down to Marseilles since the war had
begun that rented accommodation was in short supply. The kind of
big villa she wanted was common enough in Marseilles, but as
many wealthy people had moved there, those that were to let had
already been rented. After a week or so spent despairing that she
would find anything she wanted, one of the estate agents Gaby had
searching for her excitedly called her at her suite in the Noailles
Hotel, and said he had something for her to see. The Villa Maud.

Gaby had noticed this house in the past. Driving along the
Corniche outside Marseilles, one could hardly miss it, its white
stucco façade dominating a bend in the road and commanding wide
views over the sea to the Ile de Fortin and the Château d'If. In 1918

the only entrance was through tall and ornate wrought-iron gates on the road, which led into a small courtyard overlooked by a gatekeeper's lodge. From here, steps cut into the rock led onto a path, which ran beneath the fan-palms and yucca trees, under arbours of orange, pink and purple bougainvillea, and eventually reached the balustraded terrace which fronted the house. House seems an inadequate word. It was, and still is, a small château, happily combining the elegant sobriety of Second Empire neoclassical architecture with the brightly tiled and balconied gaiety of a Mediterranean villa.

It is as enchanting inside as out. An arched front door of ironwork and glass leads into a hall lined with pink and white marble pillars. The floor is a lush, delicate mosaic of lilacs, pinks and greens, a design of garlands and swags of flowers, connected and tied about with ribbons of gold and silver. Off this hall lie small but well-proportioned reception rooms; here an intimate drawing room with more pink and white marble on floors and walls; there a formal dining room panelled in pear wood. All these rooms have large windows offering views through the exotic vegetation to the Mediterranean.

Gaby wanted the house as soon as she saw it. She would have liked to buy it, but for the moment it was only for rent. She learnt from the estate agent that the house had been built thirty or forty years earlier by a rich industrialist, who had named it after his wife, and had given it to her as a wedding present.

She was impatient to move in. As soon as she did, Maman moved in with her. Whilst Gaby had been staying at her hotel, Maman had moved back into the house in the rue Tapis-Vert, but the place held too many memories for her, and she was not happy there. Gaby wondered if her mother might be a little lonely in the big, isolated Villa Maud, whether she might miss her family and friends, and the bustle of living in the centre of town where she had always lived. But Maman told her that she had spent so many of the past few years away from Marseilles that she had lost touch with most of her friends. And as for her family, she had little to do with the Caires; they had shown their disapproval of her when she had left Hippolyte to join Gaby in Paris, and she had seen nothing of them since her husband's death a few years earlier. Since Matichon had gone to live in New York after her marriage, the only close family that Maman had was her sister, Madame Quenau, and she would be delighted to come and visit the big house on the Corniche.

Meanwhile, Léon Volterra, Jacques-Charles, Harry and the *Laissez-les Tomber!* company came down from Paris. The transformation of the decrepit old Châtelet Theatre into Le Grand Casino had been effected with miraculous speed. Local publicity described it as the largest and most elegant music hall in France. As well as seating for literally thousands in the auditorium, the Casino incorporated a plush brasserie and bar, run by Monsieur Albert, a friend of Volterra's from Paris who had had thirty years' experience running some of the best-known restaurants in the capital.

Marseilles was crammed with people. Uniformed troops of every imaginable nationality thronged the boulevards, cafés and bars. La Canebière and the whole of the surrounding area buzzed with life every night almost until dawn. Every kind of entertainment was avidly sought after: the five or so music halls in the town played to packed houses; the hordes of streetwalkers sported more finery than ever before, and daily defended their territory from invading gold-diggers from all over France. Girls were converging on the city from as far away as Bordeaux, even Paris. At night the whole of the harbour area resembled a tarts' convention. There was much rivalry for the best-frequented sidewalks, and many a screaming match broke out as one of the local girls defended her patch against some brazen usurper from Paris. Though the argot of the Faubourg St Denis must have been pretty unintelligible to natives of the Canebière, neither party needed much imagination to know what the other was saying.

By the middle of October the Casino was ready, and rehearsals began in earnest. The local interest Volterra planned to inject into the show included hiring the Marseillais comedian Augé who would do an impersonation of Gaby as part of his act. She was less happy about this than she had been about Robert Hale's impersonation a few years earlier, particularly as Augé's impression included her singing and talking in the commonest imaginable local accent. She had tried for years to iron out the Provençal tones in her voice; she had even injected Anglicisms into her French following

161

her seasons in London. Unfortunately Augé had picked up on this, and his rendition of her was peppered with English words and expressions, to great comic effect.

At rehearsals, everyone found it very funny. If Gaby's amusement was tempered by a slight feeling of unease, she let it pass. Augé did, after all, profess to admire her greatly, and as everyone else seemed to find his impersonation great fun, not malicious, Gaby did not reveal that she had found it a little too well-observed, and close to the mark. Meanwhile, she was a great local heroine. Much had been made of her return to Marseilles. The local papers were having a field day. This was the 'local girl made good' story *par excellence*. The new version of *Laissez-les Tomber!* even included a scene entitled 'Gaby's return to Marseilles', and this was a theme picked up not only by the local press, but also by the posters plastered all over town announcing the revue.

Being back in Marseilles brought back many memories of her childhood, and Gaby was as happy as she had ever been. One morning before rehearsals, she even went with Maman back to the rue de la Rotonde where she had been born. They sat on a bench underneath the plane trees in the Place Jean Labadie at the bottom of the street. Gaby looked over at her mother.

'It seems like yesterday, Maman, doesn't it?'

Maman, no doubt remembering how much larger her family had been then, how many of her children she had lost, felt a lump in her throat, and got up to leave. They walked slowly over to where a crowd had begun to gather around Gaby's gleaming white Sheffield limousine, parked by the side of the square, Gaby's arm around her mother's shoulders. It was only a minute's drive to the Grand Casino. The vast theatre where the Queen of the Music Hall was due to open in triumph a few days hence was, ironically, close to the dusty square where a little girl had played thirty-seven years ago, and dreamed of being an actress.

On 4 November, Gaby gave a birthday dinner at the villa, a large affair attended by members of the company as well as one or two old family friends. She was relaxed and happy in her new home, which she laughingly referred to as *mon petit cabanon* (my little shack). Everyone agreed how well she fitted into the house, how much at ease she was in this essentially feminine environment; even the delicate marquetry and gilt furniture which it already contained could have been chosen by Gaby herself.

A few days later, on 11 November 1918, just before the revue was due to open, the Armistice was declared, and the whole town went mad with happiness and relief. No one could remember scenes of such rejoicing. Victory parades were rapidly organized, crowds of people danced in the streets, the whole of the Canebière was bedecked with the flags of the victorious Allies and huge banners bearing the portrait of President Clemenceau, the 'Father of Victory'.

In this atmosphere of fervent rejoicing, *Laissez-les Tomber!* opened on the night of Friday 14 November. Gaby had experienced many opening nights in her life, but never anything like this. As she stepped onto the stage, a huge roar went up, as over two thousand people cheered, whistled and screamed their approval. She was so touched that, by the time the applause subsided, she could barely find her voice.

'The Ladders Tableau' had been renamed 'The Ladders of Victory', and provided the climax to an evening of excitement unequalled in the history of the music hall. When the curtain came down, after seemingly endless applause, theatre staff started to carry onto the stage dozens of vast and elaborate baskets of flowers, until the whole stage was covered by them. To Gaby's stupefaction, the cards they bore all carried the same scrawled signature – 'Georges G.'

Gaby's curiosity about her mysterious admirer was satisfied the next evening when Maman brought an old business associate of Monsieur Caire's to her dressing room after the show. With him came a tall, shy young man, Georges Gatineau-Clemenceau, whose mother Thérèse Gatineau was the daughter of the most popular man in France, President Georges Clemenceau, the Father of Victory. Gaby was flattered by the attention of a member of such an illustrious family. She thanked him for all his flowers, and said that the least she could do in return was invite him to a dinner party she was planning for the following evening to celebrate the opening of the revue.

When they were all gathered at the Villa Maud the next night after the show, the guests including Volterra and Jacques-Charles, as well as Maman, Harry, Georges and his friend, Gaby realized that there would be thirteen seated at the table, a most inauspicious number. To avoid bad luck, Harry suggested laughingly that maybe he could sit at a small table, like a child at a grown-up dinner, but Gaby had a better idea. Her maid could join them. She had great fun helping the astonished girl dress up in one of her dresses, and even gave her a row of pearls to wear. Gaby's high spirits kept the evening buoyant, but there was an undercurrent of tension. Maman's dislike of Harry, which had lasted for years, was still apparent, though for Gaby's sake she tried not to let it show. Conversation, nonetheless, did not flow easily between them. Jacques-Charles recalls that he did not care for Georges, that he found him shifty and, inexplicably, untrustworthy, though his opinions at the time of writing his memoirs years later may have been coloured by the fact that in later life Georges was involved in numerous scandals, and came to be known as the black sheep of the Clemenceau family.

All in all, it was not an easy evening.

Over the next few weeks Gaby saw a great deal of Georges. Although charmed by his manners and attentions, the disparity in their ages precluded, at least for her, any serious attachment. She was practically old enough to be his mother. But he was obviously infatuated with her, so she felt that the situation had to be handled sensitively. He watched every performance of the show from his stage box, his large circle of friends leading the applause. Additionally, he thought up all sorts of elaborate and expensive schemes to please his idol. One night he had a 100 white doves released into the auditorium; another night, the startled audience was showered with the petals of thousands of pink roses. On another occasion, he arranged for the theatre to be sprayed with Gaby's favourite perfume, and distributed to the audience boxes of sweets bearing her portrait on the lid.

Gaby was enchanted by all this, and before long Georges was frequently accompanying her around town. He and his friends became regular visitors to the Villa Maud, and merry parties often went on there until the early hours, Gaby and Harry sometimes entertaining the company with impromptu songs and dances.

Gaby was in a relaxed and happy state of mind. By day she continued in her charity work, and tirelessly organized concerts and fêtes for the war-wounded. She and Harry were rapturously received at one such concert that they gave for American troops billeted at *L'American Park*, outside Marseilles. She did the rounds of the hospitals; she was photographed touring the wards of the Michel Lévy Hospital, where she brought a little joy to the lives of the hundreds of wounded men housed there. The local press gave her much coverage. Exactly as she had done in London, she threw open the door of her house to them, and gave interviews to, amongst others, Jean Tourette. To him she outlined her plans for staying in Marseilles for a while. She was considering taking up the offer of an Italian film-maker, who she did not name, to make some films in Rome in the near future. Following her usual interview tactics, personal issues were avoided. She had never revealed her inner self to the press, and she was not about to start now. Her only really candid statement to the press had been back in 1911, when she made the by-now-notorious 'Why I take all I can and give nothing back' remarks.

Perhaps she realized how much harm this had done to her image. Whatever the reason, no subsequent interviews ever hinted at her true feelings, or revealed details of her private life. Most interviewers understood that they must never ask personal questions, except, of course, those in America, where this unspoken rule was often flouted, but where she just ignored questions she found intrusive. On this occasion, in Marseilles, Jean Tourette asked her about her relationship with King Manuel. Her answer was as simple as it was enigmatic: 'You mustn't believe everything you hear on this subject. Let's just say that it's a legend that does contain a little truth . . . but only a little'.

The negative feelings that Jacques-Charles and Volterra had experienced on their first meeting with Georges Clemenceau had not changed, and consequently they played little part in Gaby's social life. Jacques-Charles was spending much time in Paris anyway, overseeing Mistinguett and Chevalier's second revue at the Casino de Paris. Aptly entitled *Boum!*, it had opened at the very end of the war, when German bombardments of Paris with their 'Big Bertha' guns were at their most ferocious.

Volterra and Gaby had never been anything other than business associates. Whilst she admired his directness, he made it quite clear that he was not impressed by her *légende*. Star or no star, he was running the show, and when it came down to brass tacks, he was her boss. Volterra had confided in Jacques-Charles that he despised Gaby's 'little set', especially Georges, whose sycophantic attitude towards Gaby he found sickening. Although the extravagant gestures that Georges thought up to please Gaby provoked his derision, Volterra was, in truth, probably a little jealous that he had not thought up these stunts himself, as they were splendid exercises in public relations, and had done much to help the show.

Laissez-les Tomber! continued to do well, and the whole troupe enjoyed great popularity in Marseilles, but after a few weeks attendances began to die down. The Grand Casino was an enormous space to fill, and for every performance to play to capacity, 20,000 people would have had to see the show each week. Volterra had not reckoned on the war finishing quite so soon. With so many troops going home, and Parisians returning to pick up the threads of their lives, the population of Marseilles, and consequently the Casino's audience, was rapidly dwindling. A huge party was thrown for the cast to celebrate the one hundredth performance in January 1919. A couple of days later, Volterra announced that the show would close on 12 February.

With its cast of hundreds, the production was just too expensive a revue to keep running to half-empty houses. Volterra planned to replace *Laissez-les Tomber!* with a smaller revue, something aimed at local business consisting of fewer foreigners and Parisians. This new show, provisionally entitled *On Y Va Tous*, he hoped would include Gaby and Harry, Dranem, Augé, Andrée Marly, and other local celebrities. Rehearsals were to start immediately.

There had been tension between Volterra and Gaby for some time. In the past, he had always been willing to take her advice in matters of production. Now, however, he was beginning to see her suggestions for the new show as criticisms, and discussions between the two often deteriorated into arguments. Gaby did not hesitate to discuss this state of affairs with her friends, and of course, they always took her side, which only exacerbated an already difficult situation. Volterra began to think that her friends were setting her up against him, and eventually the atmosphere backstage became electric. Both the rehearsals of *On Y Va Tous* by day and the performances of *Laissez-les Tomber!* by night were conducted under stressful conditions. The company seemed to be split in two; many of the cast of the old revue who were not being hired for the new one took Gaby's side.

Gaby felt that the comedian, Augé, knowing that Volterra was using him for the new show, was siding against her. On the night of 5 February 1919, she thought his parody of her was grotesque. This time he had gone too far. In his act he portrayed her painted like a waterfront whore, and talking like a fishwife. Some of the audience thought it funny, but Gaby was not amused. At the end of the performance she marched into Volterra's office to complain, and an angry exchange ensued, every syllable of which reverberated throughout the theatre.

'I'm sick to death of you and your whims and caprices,' Volterra screamed, 'You can do what you like. As far as I'm concerned, the revue is finished.'

Gaby, too, had had enough. She spent the next day making arrangements with Maman to look after the house. On the morning of 7 February, without saying goodbye to anyone, she and Harry drove to St Charles' Station and boarded the Paris Express.

18

A FATAL ATTRACTION

It seems odd that Gaby should leave Marseilles so suddenly, and with it a period of her life that appeared to hold so much promise, and, in some ways, such fulfilment. Her disagreement with Volterra was hardly reason enough for her to abandon her newly acquired home, for which she had expressed such fondness. It is possible, however, that her involvement with Georges had become more intense than she wished, and that the fight with Volterra was a good excuse to escape from it.

She had taken the Villa Maud on a long lease, therefore she must have been planning to spend more time in Marseilles than she eventually did, and, for a while at least, to use it as her home base. She had at no point considered relinquishing either her Paris home or the house in London. Both remained open and run by a skeleton staff in her absence. Indeed, she had been talking of returning to London in the near future to play in musical comedy, but it was just one of many projects that she freely discussed with everyone, including the press, most of which never reached fruition.

Gaby could, at this point in her life, have easily afforded to lead a much more leisurely existence. Her fears of being old and poor had given way merely to a fear of being old. Time and again she had stated that she would not struggle on with her career beyond middle age, as she had no wish to become a character actress. Yet the wide diversity of plans that she continued to announce both privately and publicly indicate that she felt there was still much to be accomplished, a host of ambitions to be fulfilled. Her persistent drive still prevented her from leading the easier life that her considerable wealth might have allowed.

As soon as she arrived in Paris, she was approached by Madame Rasimi to appear at the Fémina Theatre, which had been closed for the best part of the war. As a female impresario, Madame Rasimi's position in the theatre was unique. She had at various times controlled three Paris theatres: the Fémina, the Apollo and, perhaps most famously, the Ba-ta-clan. She was involved in the writing and staging of all the revues produced at these houses, even, on occasion, in making the costumes. She outlined her plans to Gaby and Harry for her re-opening of the Fémina, and they agreed to participate.

In the meantime, Jacques-Charles arrived in Paris. The night of Gaby and Volterra's big fight, Jacques-Charles had been sound asleep in his hotel room, exhausted after the journey down from Paris. He had been rudely awakened by Volterra around midnight, and summoned to the Grand Casino. Together they had worked through the whole of the next day, patching together a revue that could be staged the following night, and for the five succeeding evenings, until *On Y Va Tous* was ready to open on 12 February. It was a monumental task, but they succeeded. Jacques-Charles stayed in Marseilles until *On Y Va Tous* opened, and then made his way to Paris with a view to reconciling Gaby and Volterra, and of persuading her to come back down to reappear at the Casino. Although she received Jacques-Charles cordially enough, she had by this time signed a contract with Madame Rasimi.

Madame Rasimi planned to create a stir at the re-opening of the Fémina. She had entitled the show *La Marche à l'Etoile*, and had employed the services of a young Russian costume designer who was beginning to make a name for himself. He had worked with Paul Poiret, but his style was unique. In later years, he would become the world's leading costume designer. His name was Romain de Tirtoff, but professionally he used the name Erté, taken from the French pronunciation of his initials.

Erté lived in Monte Carlo at this time. He distinctly remembers Gaby and Harry visiting him there to discuss his designs for *La Marche à l'Etoile*. This visit must have taken place some time towards the end of February at the latest, as the revue was planned to open in April.

Erté and Gaby were mutually impressed with each other. He remembers her as being 'aussi aimable et gentille que ravissante' – 'as charming as she was beautiful'. She certainly recognized his genius, and enthused over the designs. One which particularly pleased both star and designer featured a skirt made of ermine, with two enormous trains, one either side.

In Paris Madame Rasimi was doing much to get the forthcoming show advertized. Her considerable inventive genius was called into full play. She had a series of Gaby dolls made up for sale in the foyer, and announced to the press that the stars of her new revue would be Gaby Deslys and Harry Pilcer – and a gorilla.

One day she made Gaby and Harry fly in a small aircraft, buzzing the rooftops and scattering on the heads of startled passers-by thousands of gold paper coins with their names and profiles inscribed on them. It was an exciting experience for Gaby, who had never flown before. Years before, she had wanted to make a jump from a balloon to publicize one of her shows, and only Maman's exhortations had prevented her from doing so. This time, however, Maman was out of the way, and Gaby and Harry were taken through a whole series of complicated manoeuvres by the pilot, including looping the loop.

A less amusing incident was a theft from the theatre, which caused the opening to be delayed by a week. Gaby had hoped to use some original American songs that she and Harry had recorded in New York at the end of her last disastrous trip there three years previously, but on 27 March the recording was stolen, and despite a 20,000 franc reward, it did not reappear. New material had to be found rapidly to take its place.

When the show finally opened on 8 April 1919, competition was stiff for opening-night seats in the small auditorium, many of Gaby's wealthier fans paying up to 9,000 francs for the few available boxes. The gorilla turned out to be a chimpanzee, but he caused a sensation nonetheless, especially on the night that he took fright and rushed, screeching, from the stage into the audience. The chimpanzee was not the only thing the audience had to be worried about. One critic, contrasting the smallness of the auditorium with the vastness of Gaby's headdress, said that his seat was so close to the stage that, at one point, he was afraid that if Gaby's feathered monster was not firmly anchored to her head, *he* would end up wearing it.

Erté's costumes, (for which he received no credit – the programme reads 'costumes by Madame Rasimi'), were greatly admired.

Paris was still full of American troops, and many reviewers felt that the whole revue was aimed at them – with its jazz score, English songs, and even some dialogue in English. Many French people were unhappy about this. Critics voiced the opinion that Gaby had spent too many years away from France to know what French audiences wanted; she had performed for too long in countries where eccentricity was a prerequisite of success. It seems curious that, in later years, when this revue style had become standardized, it was universally identified as French, whereas in these early days, French critics decried the style as being too American for Paris audiences.

Jacques-Charles records that Gaby was less than happy working at the Fémina. She felt restricted by the smallness of the space, and after working at the two Casinos for so long, she missed the excitement of appearing before a huge and responsive audience. The adulation of fans by the thousand had become an essential part of her life. What had started out as an instinctive need to be appreciated had developed into a full-blown love affair – the most fulfilling one she could ever experience. Of course, a performer's love affair with his or her public is as old as theatre itself. Having experienced it, many great theatrical personalities, especially women, find it hard subsequently to give sufficiently of themselves to any one person; love on a personal level frequently eludes them all their lives. Many of Gaby's contemporaries remained unattached in private life: from Polaire, who lived so totally for her performances that she had barely any existence outside of them, to others like Jenny Golder and Gaby's old school-friend, Régine Flory, whose total commitment to their careers led to an inability to find personal happiness, and eventually to suicide. For them, and eventually for Gaby, the attraction to fame proved fatal.

Of course, there were the innumerable actresses who had married wealthy or titled men and then retired from the stage, but a successful stage or film career combined with a happy marriage remained and remains a rarity. By the 1960s, the concept of the much-married Movie Queen had become a cliché, but Maurice Chevalier was writing of a much earlier generation when he said, 'In France . . . theatre queens did not marry into the milieu of lords and ladies or immensely wealthy men with whom they consorted, as this would have meant the end of the careers they loved. Nor did they marry amongst themselves . . . matrimony meant ties . . .'

Gaby's relationships, in as much as we know of them, were, with the exception of Harry Pilcer, devoid of any emotional commitment on her part. Frequently they consisted merely of Gaby handling the emotions of someone enamoured of her. One such friendship was that which she conducted with Gérard, the young Duc de Crussol. They had met in 1917 during the run of *Laissez-les Tomber!*, when friends of the Duc had taken him backstage to meet Gaby. He subsequently saw the show several times, and he and Gaby became friends. Gaby liked him, and although she doubtless found his quiet good looks and obvious breeding attractive, he was sixteen years her junior, and she did not consider him a prospective lover. This was a situation she was getting used to. When she returned to Paris in 1919 their friendship was renewed and before long it became clear that it meant a great deal more to the Duc than it did to Gaby.

The Duc came from one of the most distinguished families in France, the most famous member of which was his grandmother, the Dowager Duchesse d'Uzès, who was known as the best sportswoman in Europe. Equally at home on horseback, cycling or behind the wheel of a car, she still hunted at the age of eighty, and at the age of eighty-three became the president of the Women's Automobile Club of France. A stern matriarch, she ruled her family with a rod of iron. When items concerning the Duc's friendship with Gaby started to appear in the gossip columns, he was subjected to some censure, not only from his grandmother, but also from the rest of his family.

Gaby divided her time between Paris and Marseilles. As her lease on the Villa Maud was approaching its end, she was pleased to be able to buy the freehold for 326,000 francs (approximately £20,000), signing the agreement in the office of the Caire family lawyer, Maître Maria, on 29 July. She also managed to buy a plot of land adjoining the villa so that a driveway could be constructed that would give her car access to the front of the house. Work on this began immediately.

She was undecided about her immediate future. *Bouclette* was released in the summer and received rave reviews, fuelling Gaby's intention of exploring the cinematic medium further. Film companies in America were starting to offer long-term contracts to artists, under which quantities of rapidly made features were turned out with great precision, keeping to formulae that were considered safe and successful, but which led to many of the early stars becoming stereotyped. Under the terms of their contracts they had little say in the choice of script material, and were totally at the mercy of the studio heads. Needless to say, this scheme of things did not suit Gaby's independent spirit. She talked about setting up her own production company, but this was just another plan that did not reach fruition.

She was approached by Eclipse Films in the summer, with the script for *Le Dieu du Hasard* (The God of Luck), and was pleased with the scope offered by the central part. As well as acting, singing and dancing, she would have a chance to display her skill at swimming, and even at gymnastics. Although gymnastics are not the sort of activity that one takes up at the age of almost forty, her dancing and rigorous routine of rehearsal and classes had kept her very fit, and she was able to perform convincingly enough in the outdoor scenes for the film, which were shot on the coast at Trouville in August. Gaby and Harry were photographed on the beach and in the water, and crowds gathered to watch the filming. The talented young photographer Jacques-Henri Lartigue took photographs of the whole event. The interior scenes were to be shot in Paris later in the year. It was with a view to discussing further picture deals that Gaby planned to sail to New York in the autumn.

She took the decision to return to America despite many misgivings. Maman did not like the idea; she reminded Gaby of the bad time she had had there on her last trip, but once Gaby had made up her mind, she was a difficult person to dissuade. In September, a month or so before she planned to leave, she paid a visit to the office of Maître Maria, the lawyer, in Marseilles' rue Montgrand. She told him she was planning to do a great deal of travelling, to Italy and the United States, and that she wanted, before she left, to make a will, details of which she had already drawn up. It was as though she had had a premonition of doom. She had, after all, been travelling constantly for the last sixteen years, without having felt the need to make this kind of provision. She had made a will previously, years before in America, but that had been at the suggestion of her American lawyer friend Charlie Hanlon.

She made her way to Le Havre and set sail for New York early in October. After two days at sea, she discovered that the Duc de Crussol had stowed away on board to be near her. Once again, as she arrived in New York the press were waiting to greet her, and once again they had news for her. The Duc's mother had discovered that her son was missing, had guessed that he might be with the 'notorious' Gaby Deslys, and was following him on the next available ship.

Gaby refused to be flustered. The Duc had told the press that he was in love with her, and that he wanted her to become his wife. Gaby, ever loath to discuss her private life, was compromised into making a statement. She felt compelled to do so following American newspaper reports that she had kidnapped the eligible young Duc, who was almost young enough to be her son. She confirmed that the Duc wanted to marry her, and that he had wanted to do so since they had first met in 1917. He had repeated the proposal just before she sailed for New York. There she told reporters: 'The Duke is an elegant and kind young man, but I have no wish to be a Duchess, I prefer to work and be free. I had no idea he planned to come to America, he took the decision at the last minute and didn't even bring any baggage. I knew nothing of his presence on board until the second day out'.

Gaby stayed in New York for about three weeks. It was not a fruitful visit, and she returned without having signed any contracts. She may have been tempted to prolong the visit, but she had the interior shots for *Le Dieu du Hasard* to complete, and she was, most untypically, feeling very tired.

She had lunch in Larue's restaurant in the rue Royale with London journalist Philip Page. He asked her what plans she had for the future. She regretted feeling that she still had so much to do, and said, 'Soon it will be a struggle with time for me, and I am too tired to struggle. I can afford to rest, and wish for rest'.

She finished the interior shots for the film. In the script, Gaby is married to a wealthy but villainous financier. The film opens in semi-darkness, a maid enters the darkened bedchamber of her still-sleeping mistress. The curtains are slowly pulled back, and the light floods in to reveal Gaby lying in bed, her curly fair hair in picturesque disarray on the lace-trimmed pillow. At the end the despotic husband commits suicide, while the wife happily falls into the arms of her handsome young admirer – played by Harry, of course – who has loved her from afar.

This ending was changed at Gaby's request. After the heroine's husband's death, Gaby has the heroine writing a letter to her lover, saying that she has not much longer to live. The director, Henri Pouctal, warned her that it would make a very melancholic ending, but Gaby insisted that the film be shot that way.

Jacques-Charles had been successful in his attempts to patch up the quarrel between Gaby and Volterra. He tried to persuade her to do another season at the Grand Casino de Marseille, where they were planning a new revue to open in January, called *Ça Vaut de l'Or* ('It's Worth Gold'). Gaby told him that she had no plans for stage work, that she wanted to devote more time to making movies, and that she had signed a contract to start shooting in Italy in the New Year.

Harry had no part in these plans. He remained the closest friend she had, but from this time on their careers would take divergent paths. He was, and always had been in love with live theatre; for him movie-making just did not provide the same thrill. He was only too pleased, therefore, to take up Jacques-Charles' offer of a part in *Ça Vaut de l'Or*, and after a sad farewell to Gaby at the beginning of December 1919, he went to Marseilles to start rehearsals.

Ever since he had bought the Casino de Paris, Volterra had been casting acquisitive eyes at the Théâtre Réjane which adjoined the Casino, of which it had once formed an annexe. Réjane had retired in 1915, and his theatre had stood empty ever since. Volterra managed to acquire it, again for next to nothing. By December 1919 it had been completely refurbished, renamed the Théâtre de Paris, and was ready to open. Jacques-Charles asked Gaby and a few of her friends to the first night of the inaugural production, *La Vièrge Folle* – 'The Foolish Virgin'.

Gaby had been feeling fragile since her return from America, so much so that she had summoned Maman from Marseilles. There was nothing particularly wrong with her, just a general feeling of malaise. The night she went to the opening of the Théâtre de Paris Maman tried to dissuade her, but Gaby thought an outing would do her good. Unfortunately, dense crowds prevented her car from picking her up immediately after the show finished, and as she stood outside waiting for it, and chatting with Jacques-Charles, the heavens opened and she was drenched.

The next day she felt terrible, and did not get out of bed. Maman would have liked to call a doctor immediately, but Gaby told her that it was just a slight chill, that she would be all right in a day or two. After three days she was no better, and Maman summoned Dr Gosset, Gaby's physician. He immediately diagnosed pneumonia, and had Gaby moved to his clinic at 33, rue Antoine Chantin.

It was a protracted and painful illness. Complications developed, and a small tumour was found in Gaby's throat. Numerous attempts were made to remove it, but Dr Gosset's efforts were impeded by the fact that Gaby refused to allow the surgeon to scar her neck; so all attempts to remove the growth had to be made via her mouth. These attempts were excruciatingly painful for her; on only two occasions did she have the benefit of an anaesthetic.

Every day different visitors arrived. Gaby was frequently too unwell to see anyone, her febrile grip on reality further blurred by large doses of painkillers, and if friends came to see her she hardly knew who they were. Of all her visitors, besides Maman, just one was there every day – the Duc de Crussol.

As the new decade dawned, Gaby's condition deteriorated, and on 12 February 1920, Harry received a cable in his dressing room at the Grand Casino de Marseille, informing him of Gaby's death the previous day.

No one had told him how serious her condition had been. He felt angry and betrayed, but he went on stage that night. He danced, sang, smiled for the audience. The real actor took over, and for two hours he performed like a clockwork toy. Only later, on the night express to Paris, did the truth hit home and the tears start.

When Gaby had been lying in Dr Gosset's clinic, half conscious and barely able to talk, she had one day whispered to her mother,

'I have danced all my life for the poor'. This made little sense to poor Madame Caire, who, not wishing to tax her daughter, had let the mystery remain.

After the funeral service on 14 February, Maître Maria came to rue Henri-de-Bornier and opened Gaby's will. Apart from numerous small bequests to maids, dressers and others who had worked for her, Gaby left a life interest in the bulk of her fortune to her mother and sister, with the stipulation that they should not dispose of seventy-five per cent of it, which, after their deaths, would revert to the city of Marseilles, to be used in social service programmes to help the poor. She specified that, after her mother's death, the villa on the Corniche should be turned into a hospital for sick children in memory of her dead brother and sisters, and that this hospital should bear her name. Gaby remembered Harry with a legacy of one million francs, and an income of 1,500 francs per month for life.

Much of her property, including her jewellery, was to be sold at a later date. The total amount of her estate would depend on the results of these sales, but it was believed to be in the region of 12 million francs, approximately £400,000. It is hard to estimate how much this would amount to in today's terms, but when one considers that in 1920 the cost of a new semi-detached house was around £600, and that £10,000 would buy a mansion in Mayfair, a conservative estimate would be around £40 million.

After the reading of the will, Maman was exhausted, her mind was numb, her eyes were red and swollen with weeping and lack of sleep. For the months that Gaby had been lying sick, Maman had been constantly by her side. Dr Gosset had arranged a room for her next door to her daughter, and some nights she had rested on a small day bed in Gaby's room. She had tried to sleep, but only succeeded in dozing fitfully, always half-conscious of Gaby's presence, and the laboured breathing of her drug-induced slumber. Dr Gosset had offered to provide a nurse to sit with Gaby in case she should awaken in the night, but Maman had preferred to perform this service herself. For many days and nights, including the night that Gaby died, Maman's vigil was shared by Gérard, the Duc de Crussol. His devotion had been touching. Gaby's death had plunged him into the depths of melancholy. Maman had given him the embroidered blue silk kimono Gaby had been wearing when she died.

On the train taking the coffin to Marseilles, it was the Duc's company that Maman found consoling; Harry Pilcer's she found intrusive. She had never revised her opinion of him. Her dislike of him had spanned the years, and was now crystallized by Gaby's death. Despite all the grief he was exhibiting, Maman did not believe that he had really cared for Gaby, only that he had used her. She had heard that he had performed on the stage the night that Gaby died, and, irrespective of whether Gaby herself would have insisted that 'the show must go on', Maman saw this action as disrespectful, callous, and indicative of his true nature. She was not to know that Harry would mourn Gaby for the rest of his long life.

The train pulled into Marseilles' Gare St Charles late in the afternoon and was shunted into a special siding, where it stayed until the funeral service next morning. Maman remained on the train the whole time, in the carriage next to the coffin.

In the morning the coffin was taken off the train, and a remarkable scene presented itself. Hundreds of wreaths had been unloaded from the train, and hundreds more had arrived, until the station, with its glass roof, resembled an enormous greenhouse. The procession was slow in moving away from the station, and took some time to reach La Plaine, a large square in the centre of the city, a few minutes' walk from rue de la Rotonde where Gaby was born. A large public service had been organized there, so that the people of Marseilles could bid farewell to their heroine. Several thousand were gathered, despite the rain that had begun to fall.

It was a long way to the St Pierre Cemetery on the northern borders of the town, but hundreds of mourners followed the procession on foot. Behind Maman, Matichon and Harry, the mourners were led by a small group of students from the Conservatoire de Musique. The funeral bier was followed by a small donkey. It was a theatrical yet touching gesture, of which Gaby would have approved.

The cemetery of St Pierre covers an area of several square kilometres on a hill overlooking the city and the bay beyond it. Gaby's tomb lies in a quiet corner, off an avenue of magnolia trees.

A white marble column, perhaps eighteen feet high, rises in majestic simplicity against the blue southern skies that she loved so much. Her profile, complete with pearl necklaces, is carved on the front of the column, and she smiles up at the sun, her hair falling loose and curling to her shoulders.

19
A MACABRE AND RIDICULOUS JOKE

All through the 1920s Gaby's name continued to engender publicity. Just a few days after her funeral, Jean Bernard of the Brussels *Soir* published the story of the Navratil family, and their old claim that Gaby was their daughter. They said that their daughter, Hedwige, had been adopted by the Caire family after their own daughter, Gabrielle, had died. This child, known as Gabrielle Caire, but in reality Hedwige Navratil, grew up to become Gaby Deslys. This unlikely, indeed fantastic, tale was greeted with mocking derision in France, where few newspapers bothered to print it. It did, however, gain some credence in other countries; one or two obituaries of Gaby even gave her real name as Hedwige Navratil. Britain's *News of the World* wrote: 'It was a little-known fact that she was Austro-Hungarian by birth'. Gaby's reluctance to talk about her personal life had, once again, resulted in the general public being presented with all kinds of bizarre fiction dressed up as fact.

It would seem that Madame Navratil genuinely believed that Gaby was her daughter. The story of her being adopted by the Caire family was nonsense, but the history of the claim goes back so far in Gaby's career that it is evident that it was not just a question of fake relatives turning up after a rich woman had died. The Navratils had believed Gaby to be their daughter even before she had made any money, and now that there was 12 million francs at stake, they became even more determined to prove it.

They were helped in this by an extraordinary, and to this day unexplained, coincidence. They claimed that their daughter Hedwige was born on 30 October 1885. Gaby Deslys' death certificate states that she was born on exactly the same day. Gaby Deslys' *birth* certificate, however, states quite plainly that she was born on 4 November 1881. How had this discrepancy occurred? It can be explained in part by the fact that Gaby had subtracted a few years from her age on her debut in Paris at the age of twenty-one. The details on the death certificate had been taken by Madame Caire's lawyer from private papers at Gaby's Paris house; papers on which she had obviously altered the date. The fact that Gaby was guilty of the very human vanity of wanting to appear younger than her years is a matter of trifling insignificance, but the real puzzle is why she should have changed the date from 4 November to 30 October – the birthdate of the mysterious Hedwige Navratil.

Whilst these curious revelations were making very short news items throughout 1920 and 1921, Madame Caire did the best she could to sort out her own life. She needed a rest more than anything, and for several weeks after Gaby's death she shut herself up in the Villa Maud, now re-named the Villa Gaby, with Matichon and her husband for company if she wanted it. They had come over from New York when Gaby was taken into the clinic, and from this time on would divide their time between France and the United States. Maman was totally exhausted. She was too tired to supervise the disposal of much of Gaby's estate, and the jewellery did not come up for sale until 28 June 1920. The sale took place at the Hotel Drouot in Paris. The prices fetched were in some cases disappointing, and less than pre-sale estimates, but nevertheless the 1 million francs (approximately £11,000) that Gaby's three favourite rows of pearls fetched was still a considerable sum – enough to have bought that mansion in Mayfair, or a street of suburban semis. One of the principal bidders at this auction was Harry Pilcer, who spent nearly half the money that Gaby had left him on some very expensive mementoes.

More than a year passed before the contents of the house in Kensington Gore were disposed of. Dealers and collectors had a marvellous time, and paid nearly £50,000 for Gaby's enormous and varied collection of pictures – including some Old Masters that would today be worth millions – her Persian rugs, and mountains of bric-a-brac. Crowds of eager and curious buyers trampled through the rooms that had been featured in *Vogue* and *Tatler*. The famous bed created great interest, and stiff bidding rapidly pushed its price up to £500. The sale had been delayed until Maman felt well enough to face the journey to London to remove anything she felt was too personal to go under the auctioneer's hammer. She wanted very little from the house; the large Madonna from Gaby's bedroom was one of the few things she chose to have shipped back. The lease of the house was then sold.★

Throughout the 1920s the Navratils continued to press their claims, and hired a whole battery of detectives and lawyers to assist them. Dozens of other claimants jumped on the bandwagon, including twenty-four other Navratils who all thought that they deserved a share of Gaby's fortune. All these claims were chronicled to a greater or lesser degree by the world's press, and the stories kept re-emerging until 'The True Identity of Gaby Deslys' assumed the status of a popular soap opera. Following a pattern set in her lifetime, the press printed all sorts of wild stories about Gaby based on these claims, stories which were by no means restricted to the sensation-seeking tabloids. In 1925, even the comparatively sober *New York Times* stated:

> 'Gaby, who always endeavoured to conceal her real identity, giving herself out as French, was in reality a Slovakian peasant girl. This was first discovered by the detective who was engaged by one of Gaby's imperial admirers to find out the truth of her much disputed nationality. Gaby started her career as a servant girl called Hadwiga Navrati (sic) but forsook her family. When later the detectives brought her old mother to see the, by then famous, dancer, Gaby denied the relationship, and paid the woman a large sum to stay away.'

In 1927 the Navratil's other daughter, Madame Werkes, joined in her family's crusade, and contacted numerous newspaper offices to publicize the story further. She stated that she and her family were taking steps to press their claims according to the Hungarian laws of inheritance. Madame Caire at no point made any statement regarding these claims, obviously considering the whole thing, as did the French press, a macabre and ridiculous joke.

★ 12A Kensington Gore was demolished in 1959 to make way for the new Royal College of Art.

Harry Pilcer, who had from 1920 made his home in Marseilles, told the *Daily Chronicle*:

> 'Ever since Gaby's death there have been any number of people who have written to me saying they were sisters, brothers, mothers or fathers of my great friend, and if all their claims were true the family from which she sprang must have been quite prolific. People seem to have gone quite mad over this thing. I even had one woman writing to me trying to make an appointment so that I could hear Gaby talking from the spirit world.'

The French laws of inheritance state that any claims on an estate must be instituted within ten years of the decease. Consequently, 1929 saw a flurry of activity from the Navratil family. This time, detective agencies working for them disclosed certain facts that, nearly ten years after her death, made Gaby once again headline news around the world. These agencies published a statement from so-called official sources in Hungary, which said that the Hungarian government had issued in 1915 a warrant for the arrest of 'a young Hungarian citizen called Hedwige Navratil, otherwise known as Gaby Deslys. The young woman was sentenced in default for espionage'.

This sensational turn of events made even the French papers sit up and take notice. That one of their national heroines might have been a Hungarian was a ridiculous conjecture; that she might have masqueraded as such for the purpose of espionage was a different matter altogether. 'Gaby Deslys a Spy for the Allies', blared headlines all over the world. 'How Gaby Deslys Worked for France,' screamed the Paris tabloids. *La Liberté* conducted its own enquiry, as did the *Daily Telegraph* in London. The *Telegraph* said: 'The revelations from the Prague correspondent of the *Daily Telegraph* showing that a warrant was issued for the arrest of Gaby Deslys on a charge of having acted as a spy for the Allies during the war has led to another interesting statement. The *Liberté* tonight says that a second warrant for her arrest, issued by the Préfecture of Police at Prerau, was followed by repeated interrogations of the friends and family of Hedwige Navratil'.

One of the effects of this sensational discovery was to flush out of hiding in Biarritz a woman who bore a strong resemblance to Gaby Deslys. Her name was Hedwige Navratil. It is inexplicable why she had taken so long to show herself. She claimed that she had tried to contact her parents many times, but that her letters had always been returned unopened. She was able to prove her identity, and told her parents that they must stop all their claims to the Deslys fortune, as they would only lead to disappointment.

Although her appearance meant the end of the Navratil claims, it did nothing to clear up the mystery of the alleged espionage activities of someone who bore the names of both Hedwige Navratil and Gaby Deslys. The mystery was added to when it was discovered that a Paris theatrical directory called *Bottin Mondain*, which annually published details of performers working in France, had listed from 1915 on that Gaby Deslys was the stage name of one Hedwige Navratil.

Even in the face of this storm, Madame Caire maintained total silence. Harry Pilcer told the *Daily Chronicle*: 'The whole story is nonsense. Of course Gaby was not a spy. Our relationship as artists was of the closest until her death. If she had been a spy she would have had to resort to complicated manoeuvres to conceal her activities from me.'

Eventually a statement purporting to come from the chief of French intelligence agencies during the war was released to the press. This categorically denied that either Gaby Deslys or Hedwige Navratil was employed by the French army to seek information. Hedwige Navratil had, as a dancer, travelled all over Europe from 1905 on. To her dying day, she persisted in the belief that Gaby had used her name and taken advantage of their strong resemblance to perform all sorts of undercover activities. Although this seems unlikely, the truth behind the matter has never been satisfactorily resolved. The fact remains that the date of birth on Gaby Deslys' death certificate is indeed that of Hedwige Navratil, and there is no logical explanation why *Bottin Mondain* should give Hedwige Navratil as Gaby Deslys' real name.

The greatest mystery of all would appear to be that of Gaby's Croix de Geurre. There exist numerous references – in Jacques-Charles' memoirs, for example – to Gaby having been decorated by the French Government at the conclusion of World War One.

Jacques-Charles wrote of a visit to Madame Caire some time after Gaby's death. Maman showed him: '. . . finally the Diploma of "Caporal" Gaby Deslys, and her Cross, accompanied by letters from two of the greatest Marshals of France, attesting to the fact that "Caporal Gaby Deslys has well earned the glory of her Motherland".★ I promised to maintain a respectful silence about this admirable secret, and I will not divulge it now.'

These letters, from Marshal Joffre and Marshal Foch, are referred to time and time again in French newspapers of the 1920s, without any details of what Gaby had done to earn this honour, and Jacques-Charles never did divulge the 'admirable secret'. Even though Gaby's decoration seems to have been well-documented in the 1920s, in 1986 official sources in France will neither confirm nor deny its existence. If the French government saw fit to reward Gaby with a decoration for her tireless efforts at recruiting and entertaining the wounded, there would surely be no reason for their withholding this information. However, I was told that information regarding decorations for any kind of intelligence work are never divulged, even if such information concerns a period as historically remote as World War One. So the mystery remains.

Maman Caire's resentment of Harry Pilcer proved long-lasting, even vindictive. Harry brought to Gaby's funeral a beautiful bronze palm to be placed permanently on her tomb, but it was 'lost' by Maman. In 1921 Maman announced that she would contest Gaby's legacy to Harry. It is hard to imagine on what grounds she hoped to bring this action, even though nothing ever came of it. Presumably she had second thoughts.

She became increasingly bitter as time went on. She obtained no joy from Gaby's money, and devoted a great deal of time to fighting real and imagined claims against it. Gaby wished for a large mausoleum to be erected on land that she had purchased at the time of her father's death. Madame Caire commissioned Professor Carli of the École de Beaux Arts in Paris to design something suitable, and he set about making elaborate scale models to show her. She selected a design, and Professor Carli told her it would cost approximately 500,000 francs to build. She was so infuriated with

★Coporal Gaby Deslys a bien mérité de la Patrie.

this estimate that she cancelled the whole plan, and Professor Carli had to sue her for the 80,000 francs he estimated his work had already cost. The mausoleum was never built. Gaby rests in the tomb that she had built for her father, and the extra land she bought for her mausoleum is planted with geraniums.

In 1921 officials of the city of Marseilles approached Maman, suggesting that as Gaby obviously wanted to help the sick and poor of the City, the Villa Gaby should be sold immediately, and the money used to purchase a plot of land more suitable for a hospital. The villa, being high on its cliff, was hardly convenient for the purpose, they said. Madame Caire refused this suggestion. She lived alone in her beautiful villa until 1929, when failing health forced her to move to Cannes, to a villa called Mont-Joli, in the Californie district. Matichon and her husband returned to France to look after her. Maman died in Cannes in 1936 after a long illness. Only then was the Villa Gaby taken over by the city of Marseilles and turned into the School of Hydrography. It was used to house troops in the Second World War, and is currently in use as a hostel for medical research students from overseas.

Gaby never got her hospital.

Soon after Gaby's funeral, Gérard, Duc de Crussol, sailed for America on the liner *Savoie*. When interviewed on arrival, he said:

> 'Nobody in America understood Gaby Deslys. She was a beautiful soul, and whilst she loved America, the people of this country only knew of her what they read in the papers. Many of these articles were grossly untrue. There are few persons who know what she did for the poor widows and children of Frenchmen killed or wounded during the terrible war. My mother realised at last the love I had for Gaby Deslys after I left France this time, and sent me a message by wireless offering me her sympathy.'

Within three years the Duc was married.

Harry Pilcer made France his permanent home. In the early part of the 1920s he had a seventh-floor flat on the chic Avenue de Tourville in Marseilles, and he became a familiar and much-loved figure on the French music-hall and nightclub scene. He also acted as agent for numerous American artists touring in Europe. For many years before the Second World War he had his own nightclub in Paris. He spent a good part of the war in America, and in 1945 he appeared in the very successful film version of Somerset Maugham's *The Razor's Edge*.

In 1947 he planned to produce a film version of Gaby Deslys' life story, with his old friend and dance-partner, Claire Luce, taking the leading rôle. Nothing came of this plan, and Harry returned to a life of relative obscurity. In his later years, he worked as resident entertainer and compère in numerous clubs and casinos in the South of France. For many years he paid regular visits to Gaby's tomb, leaving bouquets of lilies or orchids there when he did so. Visitors to his flat in Marseilles, and to many of his subsequent homes, were shown a small room that he kept in Gaby's memory, containing photographs and flowers and a large portrait of the friend he had lost, and who had done so much to shape his life. He retained his youthful appearance well into old age, and worked right up to his death. He collapsed soon after leaving the stage of the Ambassadors Casino in Cannes on the night of 14 January 1961, at the age of seventy-six. Claire Luce remembers him well, as an attractive and good-humoured man, full of energy and *joie de vivre*. The only time she ever saw him look sad was if someone mentioned Gaby Deslys.

Ever since the public and unseemly wrangle over her fortune ceased in 1930, Gaby has vanished from the public eye. Later, in 1930, she made headlines for one final time when thieves tried to break into her mausoleum, no doubt in the hope that she had, like the queens of ancient Egypt, been buried with a fortune in jewels. Their attempts were foiled by the six-inch-thick steel plate that protects her coffin. Since then she has been left alone.

EPILOGUE

It seems ironic and a little unjust that a woman who in life, and for a while in death, was the focus of so much public attention, should be so totally forgotten. Theatrical fame is by its very nature ephemeral. The development of film has gone a long way towards preserving for posterity the public's taste in entertainers but, of course, such tastes change as rapidly as any fashion.

Little visual record remains of any of the great theatrical stars of the early part of this century. Gaby's selectivity with regard to making films has worked against her, and her chances of achieving lasting fame. So too has the nature of her success. Perhaps Mistinguett was right when she said that Gaby had very little talent in the accepted sense. Hers was a *succès de scandale* based on personality, a success of the kind that would have ensured her immortality had it only come a few years later, when the movies made stars out of such unlikely material as Jean Harlow, Norma Shearer and Joan Crawford, to name but a few, none of whose lack of talent stood in the way of their achieving enduring fame. Katherine Hepburn was asked in a recent interview what she thought it took to make a star. She replied that it had nothing to do with talent; that it was a combination of charisma and luck. Gaby undoubtedly possessed lashings of both. Had she had more of a film career, she would have achieved immortality. As it is, she lives on only in the memory of a generation that has, like her, for the best part vanished.

Cecil Beaton, who so often 'proudly declared himself to be of the Gaby Deslys period',* made a better attempt than any at keeping

---

*From *Cecil Beaton* by Hugo Vickers.

that memory alive. In his first published book, *The Book of Beauty* (1930), he enthuses wildly over her whole style and personality, and implies that she practically invented glamour and sex appeal in the modern sense. His further chapter on her in *The Glass of Fashion*, published twenty-four years later, echoes his adulation, and hints at her mysteriousness, but he can cast no light on her real character, which eluded him as it has everyone else.

All the publicity in which she revelled and to some extent propagated, and the myths and legends that grew up as a result of it, serve only to obscure even further the real personality behind the public face of Gaby Deslys. For those that lived in her time, her life had the aura of a fireworks display, a series of breathtaking explosions of light and colour, that went on for years, seeming to reach a crescendo of brilliant luminosity, and that suddenly, without warning, stopped dead.

Later, like fireworks, Gaby was hard to recreate in the mind's eye; it was hard to believe she ever really happened. Some lucky ones, like Cecil Beaton, were left with the memory of something extraordinary, the real nature of which neither he nor anyone else could explain.

Gaby Deslys remains an enigma.

INDEX

A Fleur de Peau, 15
A la Carte, 79, 81, 83, 99
Aladdin, 19–23, 26
Alfonse, 72
Amelie, Queen, 34–5, 37, 51–2
Angelsey, Lady, 108
Au Music Hall, 17
Augé, 161–2, 166–7
Augustine Victoria, Princess, 89

Baker, Josephine, 152
Bakst, Leon, 77–8
Ballets Russes, 77
Barrie, Sir James, 85–7, 101, 105, 106, 107–11, 128
Barton, Vera, 26
Bayes, Norah, 96
Beaton, Cecil, 33, 40, 79, 81, 111, 112, 189–90
Bébé, 117, 120
The Belle of Bond Street, 94
Bennett, Arnold, 108
Beretta, Raphael, 144
Berlin, Irving, 118, 121
Bernard, Jean, 180
Bernard, Sam, 94, 96
Bernel, Charles, 50
Bernhardt, Sarah, 135–6
Berny, Jules, 12–13
Binot, Jules, 6
Bishop, Fred, 29
Bishop, Will, 22, 23, 25, 28, 31
Boucicault, Dion, 109
Bouclette, 158, 172–3
Boum!, 165
Bradley, Arthur, 134

Brett, Maurice, 18
Brice, Fanny, 74
Buckingham, Rosalie Amelia, 105
Butt, Alfred, 63, 65, 67, 68, 71, 80–3, 85, 101, 106, 128, 130
Byng, Douglas, 81

Ça Vaut de l'Or, 175
Caire, Aimée (GD's sister), 2, 3, 4
Caire, Anna 'Maman' (GD's mother), 1–4, 16–17, 25, 28, 52, 65, 72, 75, 123, 127, 135, 145, 160–4, 170, 173, 175–8, 181–2, 185–6
Caire, Hippolyte (GD's father), 1–3, 4, 16, 106, 125, 127, 162
Caire, Léon (GD's brother), 2–3
Caire, Léon (GD's uncle), 1
Caire, Marie-Thérèse (GD's sister), 2
Caire, Matichon 'Kerville' (GD's sister), 2, 16–17, 39–40, 65, 112, 127, 135, 181, 186
Campbell, Mrs Patrick, 101
Campton, Aimée, 14
Les Caprices de Suzette, 30, 38
Carli, Professor, 185–6
Carrick, Hartley, 103, 128
Chaplin, Charlie, 95
Charles, Ernest, 67
Charlot, André, 39, 47–50, 63, 114, 115–16, 117, 138
Chase, Pauline, 108
Chevalier, Maurice, 154–5, 156, 165, 171–2
Chichine, 72, 83
Churchill, Lady Gwendoline, 108
Les Cloches de Corneville, 27–8

191

Cocteau, Jean, 152
Colette, 9, 41
Collins, José, 59–60
Conill, Fernand-Oscar de, 127
Conservatoire de Musique, Marseilles, 4
Cornuché, 13
Cottens, Victor de, 17
Coverdale, Minerva, 131
Crispi, Ida, 71
Crook, John, 109
Cukor, George, 33

Dale, Alan, 60, 63
D'Alençon, Emiliènne, 9, 11, 14–15
Dare, Zena, 18
Darewski, Herman, 109
Darewski, Max, 130
Davies, George Llewelyn, 108
Davies, Marion, 94, 121
Déarly, Max, 25, 26, 62
Les Débuts de Chichine, 50–1, 54, 57, 69
Diaghilev, Sergei, 77
Le Dieu du Hasard, 173, 174–5
Dillingham, Charles, 118, 121–3, 126
Dillon, Bernard, 88
Dirys, Jeanne, 14
Djeli, Sahari, 78
Dolly, Jenny, 74, 92, 147
Dolly, Rosie, 147
Doucet, 40
Douglas, Gilbert, 123
Dranem, 166
Drian, Etiènne, 79
Du Maurier, Guy de, 107, 108
Duncan, Isadora, 104
D'Uzès, Duc, 11
D'Uzès, Duchesse, 11, 172, 174

Edward, Prince of Wales, 10
Edward VII, King, 19, 27, 31, 35, 38
Edwardes, Georges, 18–20, 22
Ellice, Winifred, 132
Elsie, Lily, 51, 77

Eltinge, Julian, 71
Erté, 169–70
Eulenberg, Count von, 31
Everybody's Doing It, 71

Famous Players, 96, 97
Ferdinand of Bulgaria, 31
5064 Gerrard, 114–117
Flers, P. L., 33
Flory, Régine, 3–4, 171
Foch, Marshal, 185
Follow the Crowd, 128
Fortuny, 40
Fox, Harry, 74, 92, 121
Frohman, Charles, 110–11

Gaby, 158
Gatineau-Clemenceau, Georges, 163–164, 165, 166, 168
Georges-Michel, Michel, 155
Gérard, Duc de Crussol, 172, 174, 176, 177–8, 186
Gerrard, Teddie, 105, 116, 122, 128
Golder, Jenny, 171
Gosset, Dr, 176, 177
Gould, Frank J., 100
Grossmith, George Jr, 18–19, 71
The Guide to Paris, 71
Guilbert, Yvette, 24
Guitry, Lucien, 7
Guitry, Sacha, 7

Hale, Binnie, 116
Hale, Robert, 71, 115, 116
Hallam, Basil, 103–4
Hampe, Fritz, 45
Hanlon, Charlie, 94, 173
Hearst, William Randolph, 121
Held, Ann, 24, 54
Hepburn, Audrey, 33
Hepburn, Katherine, 189
Her Triumph, 97–8, 118, 140
Hervil, 157
Hoffman, Gertrude, 92, 93, 94
The Honeymoon Express, 74–5, 80

Infatuation, 158
Irving, H. B., 82
Isola brothers, 142

Jacques-Charles, 12, 51, 69, 71, 140–7, 149–54, 156–8, 161, 163–6, 175–6, 184
Janis, Elsie, 101
Joffre, Marshal, 185
Jolson, Al, 59, 63, 67, 74

Karsavina, 77
Keep Smiling, 90
Kern, Jerome, 109
Kerville, *see* Caire, Matichon
Kill that Fly, 71
Kolb, Marie-Thérèse, 7, 8, 12

Laissez-les Tomber!, 149–56, 161–4, 166, 172
Landolff, 79
Langtry, Lillie, 31
Lartigue, Henri, 173
Lauder, Harry, 92, 93, 95
Leopold II, King of the Belgians, 11, 31, 32
Lepkovitch, Peter, 7
Leslie, Peter, 93
Levey, Ethel, 106, 108
Lillie, Beatrice, 115
Linder, Max, 101
Lindsay, Mrs George, 77
The Little Parisienne, 91
Lloyd, Marie, 24, 28, 88
Loftus, Cissie, 108
Lorrain, Jean, 10, 13
Luce, Claire, 187
Lucile, 40

McDonald, Elizabeth, 132–4, 135–6
Mackail, Denis, 87, 107, 109–10
Mackintosh, Alastair, 103
McQueen-Pope, W., 130–1
Mademoiselle Chic, 68–9
Mademoiselle Zuzu, 129, 130

Maison Lewis, 54, 55
Manners, Lady Diana, 108
Manuel II, King of Portugal, 34–7, 38, 40, 42–5, 47, 51–2, 67, 80, 155, 165
La Marche à l'Étoile, 169–71
Marinelli, H. B., 39, 52, 118, 123–4, 125–6
Marly, Andrée, 166
Mata Hari, 78, 137
Mercanton, 157
Mérode, Cléo de, 24, 31
Millar, Gertie, 19–20, 22
Milton, Billy, 128
Mistinguett, 62, 152, 154–6, 165, 189
Monckton, Lionel, 19, 22
Monkman, Phyllis, 115
Morton, Charles, 67
Moul, Alfred, 27, 28, 39, 47–50, 63, 65, 114, 156
The Music Cure, 101
M'zelle Chichi, 14

Navratil, Hedwige, 180–1, 182–4
Navratil, Madame, 41, 137, 180
Navratil family, 180, 182–4
Négis, André, 7
Nesbit, Evelyn, 91–2
The New Aladdin, 22
Nijinsky, 77

Olchanevsky, Ben, 137–8
On Y Va Tous, 166–7, 169
Orléans, Duke of, 51
Otèro, Caroline, 9–11, 39, 41

Page, Philip, 174
Paquin, 40, 79
Paravicini, Madame, 12
La Parisienne, 45
The Passing Show, 101
Patricia, Princess of Connaught, 37
Pavlova, Anna, 77, 104
Perrey, Annie, 33
Philomene, 45
Pilcer, Elsie, 123, 125

Pilcer, Harry, 62–7, 70–3, 79, 83–4, 94, 96, 100–1, 103, 105, 116, 122–3, 125–6, 131, 134, 146, 148, 149, 151–152, 155, 156–7, 164–5, 169–70, 173, 175–8, 181, 183–7
Poiret, Paul, 40, 78, 80, 85, 169
Polaire, 12, 38, 171
Pouctal, Henri, 175
Pougy, Liane de, 9, 10–11

The Rajah's Ruby, 103, 105
Rasimi, Madame, 168–70
Raucourt, Jules, 116
Reid, Hal, 96
Réjane, 38, 175
Reutlinger, 66
Rhodes, Stanley, 18
Richter, Count von, 31
Roshanara, 78
Robey, George, 39, 63
Rosy Rapture, 108–11
Russell, Mabel, 18
Rutland, Duchess of, 108

Sans Rancune, 33–6, 49
Santley, Joseph, 121, 122
Selfe, Judge, 138–9
Selfridge, Gordon, 104–5, 107, 109, 112, 121, 128, 140, 147
Shaw, George Bernard, 82, 83, 85, 101
Shea, Jerry, 71–2
Shubert, J. J., 39, 52–4, 55–6, 57, 63, 71, 74, 88, 91–2, 93–5
Shubert, Lee, 39, 52–4, 55, 57, 63, 71, 74, 88, 91–2, 93–5
Signoret, 157
Sitwell, Osbert, 83–4
The Social Whirl, 74
Soldene, Emily, 35
Son Altesse l'Amour, 29
Sorel, Cécile, 66
Spinelly, 34, 99

Stewart-Richardson, Lady Constance, 77
Stop! Look! Listen!, 121, 122–3, 126, 128
Storey, Sylvia, 18
Sullivan, 95
Suzette, 130–2, 140, 145, 146–7

Tanguay, Eva, 92–3, 126
Tarling, Ditty, 132
Thaw, Harry K., 91
Thaw, Russell, 91
Thenon, Georges, 33
Thompson, Sir Basil, 137
Tourette, Jean, 165
Tout en Rose, 45
Tree, Sir Herbert, 101
Trefusis, Mrs, 108

Vera Violetta, 54, 57–63
La Vierge Folle, 175
Volterra, Léon, 142–7, 149–50, 154, 156–8, 161, 163, 165–7, 168–9, 175

Wagne, George, 41
Watch Your Step, 118, 121
Werkes, Madame, 182
West, Mae, 63
White, Lee, 115
White, Stanford, 91
Wilhelm, Crown Prince, 31
Wilhelm II, Kaiser, 31
Willy, Louise, 69
Wimperis, Arthur, 103, 128
Woodings, Mrs, 134
Wright, Fred, 29, 32, 56

Y a des Surprises, 8
Yukio-Tani, 20

Ziegfeld, Florenz, 24, 52–3
Zukor, Adolph, 96, 97